The Many Faces of Self Esteem

The Stepchild of Human Development

Authored By
Joanne Salsbury

ISBN: 0-6155-4276-X
ISBN-13: 9780615542768

TABLE OF CONTENTS

I am one with the music. It opens my paths of free

flowing energy. I do not ever want to separate from the

sounds which are beautifully composed. The maestro's

of music, the genius of the gifted which invade every

part of our senses. Allow music to bring out the

gifts born to us. Allow the people who read my words to

feel the logic and passion they have lost or misplaced.

Allow everyone to know what they read makes the

most sense with a subtle understanding which they

know not why, they just know they know.

Joanne Salsbury

Coprighted October 19, 2000

ACKNOWLEDGEMENTS

I would like to extend my regards to all people who have touched my life in the smallest way conceivable. To the person who gave me a dime in the checkout line when I was short-changed to the people who had significant impact in changing the way I think and act today.

I would like to thank specific people who helped me when I was down and out and needed an uplifting hand when they certainly were not responsible for my situation. I hope they receive rewards 100 fold over for their unselfish and unconditional kindness. My late mother, Ruth Salsbury, was a great support and role model in many ways, the late William McGrane, and Timothy Thayer, who mentored me though the most difficult part of my life.

Also, I would like to thank my family, my late father Elmer, my brothers, John E. and Robert A. Salsbury who never let on whether they believed or not that I would actually write any books. Each provided a myriad of challenges growing up which strengthened my core soul to make it through the worst parts of today's world.

My undying faith and trust in God allowed me to walk to the edge and peer over but never let me fall to the other side. For being my true best friend and guiding me to where I needed to be and who I needed to be with at the time I needed it the most. For the beautiful creations he has given us, the ability to have choices and compassion for all who struggle to achieve contentment. We can one day feel the energies of every living creature flow through us as one life source.

INTRODUCTION

I was standing on top of Birdrock looking over the dark crystal blue turquoise Pacific Ocean, which was calmly pulling the shore to its bosom. The water was foaming over the rocks, eroding the stones into new shapes with each wave. The breeze was so light you barely felt it pass over your body. The sun was bright and sounds of the sea lions basking in the sun's warmth gave you a feeling the worst of the winter storms were over and everyone could relax and anticipate the newness of the spring.

The peace that comes with the sounds and smells of the ocean commonly spawn introspection at the highest level. Usually, one of our questions is "What have we achieved with our lives to this point?" "How far have we come, how far do we have to go, what other surprises, good or bad, are in store for us?" Are the answers somewhere out there where we cannot ever reach or attain?

I, too, stood there feeling I have come through some tight spots, which I could not believe I actually survived mentally. I was so sure I knew what path was right for me and before I knew it, I was being forced to go another way, make new choices and decisions, which changed everything for me. I felt so far removed from what I originally planned for myself, I couldn't decide whether to be excited in anticipation of the newness coming my way or afraid I was so lost, giving up was looking like the only alternative I had left. I added to my own worry because I did not know how to give up either. So, I was a jumbled mess looking up out of this deep hole with little strength left to climb out and no apparent tools that have worked for me thus far.

I tried acting on the advice of other people, which I always kicked myself for in the end. I attempted to look for the knight in shining armor that ended up putting me farther back in the hole. I tried new environments and jobs, but was still feeling emptiness inside with no purpose left, no visible direction to go and convinced the intelligence I had was my own delusion. So, why couldn't I let go? Why couldn't I end it? What is the missing piece or peace for me?

PROLOGUE

Self Esteem has always been the stepchild of human development. We tap dance around all of the problems people have with illness, relationship and communication issues and it never seems to fall specifically on development of one's self esteem. It is posed as a need for assertiveness, self-improvement, or self-help. It is broken down into having depression, dysfunction, addictions, co-dependency and the like. When all of this is boiled together, it actually comes down to having high or low self-esteem.

It has always been somewhat taboo to use the word self esteem for very long when identifying an issue of dysfunction. Immediately it is turned into another category as I have mentioned above. I believe the reason for this is because it is actually a scary term. Self Esteem means getting down into the core of someone's feelings, which is a very protected area. Some people have suppressed feelings for one reason or another and the thought of unleashing anything that might make us feel out of control for a period is scary. There is also the problem that we have inherited someone else's self esteem and the thought that our perceptions of someone we need approval from could have flaws is overwhelming. So not only do we have our feelings to deal with, we have to face the fact our family or friends may have issues as well.

There is much "masking" out in the world to keep people off guard to what they may truly be feeling inside. This can extend from world leaders to a teacher or a boss. Through my own voracious thirst for figuring all of this out, I decided to try and put this into layman's terms that each person can relate through *feeling* what I am saying. I am convinced that self-esteem is the key to healing thyself. It encompasses your physical, mental and spiritual balances. It is a simple result, but not easy of course. If you change yourself for the better, the world will change in tandem. As you can see, the world is out of control with itself. It is a perfect time for an malevolent leader to say all the right things and everyone follows. If you begin development of your own esteem, no one will be able to lead you into an immoral direction.

www.speakersfortheworld.com

Other publications: ***Obtaining the Pearl***

Chapter 1
Your Missing Peace

What is your missing piece or peace? It is obvious to me the world is in a state of chaos and the chaos is coming from within rather than externally. The external results we see are only a mirror of what is transpiring on the inside of each one of us. If we believe that the same energy force connects all people, then the reality is a multitude of short circuits occurring which is inhibiting the smooth flow of positive energy. We become blinded to what we are truly seeking. We are seeking many external things and yet when we achieve them, we continue to feel empty. We ultimately are seeking love, to be loved, to be respected, to have a distinct and individual purpose for ourselves and to make sense of why we are alive.

What has prompted me to write this book is the experience of seeing friends, patients in psychiatric hospitals and not to exclude my own journey, struggling to hold onto life. It is that simple. The numbers are growing of people overdosing on drugs and alcohol, people cutting on themselves and others for pleasure, tasting blood because it tastes good for it is the only thing that makes sense in their lives! Is this the coming phase of extracurricular actives? Look at the people who see their external body for what is truly there. People have parties lighting cigarettes and candles to burn spots on their skin because they like to watch the skin separate and close. Is this a new science project in biology? They pierce every part of their body because of the sensations they say they feel. I knew someone who pierced one part of her body so many times;

she became lifeless in that area. She could feel nothing in the end as the initial goal was to insure she could feel something. They fail to see they are actually killing the nerve endings put into our body so we can feel pain.

The unfortunate part is these people are actually intending to feel the pain to know they are alive. They do not realize they have shut themselves off to feeling any pain from the *emotional* inside of their body. They are so fearful of the pain and the overwhelming and uncontrollable dam of suppressed emotions, that death and/or mutilation are their preferred avenues of escape. They want to know they can still feel at all or otherwise, they want release totally from the human body where they think they will find their peace.

What about the pain of feeling emotions? It can be devastating and there is no question about that issue. As a child, every growing pain experienced is verbalized and acted out a volume that could crack your eardrums. By God, they experience it, live it, feel it, and they live through it to go back and do it again or venture to the next new experience. They usually bounce back quickly, sometimes within minutes if diverted by a positive decoy. So, what does that say about the adolescent or adult? Somewhere along the line, they have been conditioned to withhold expression or emotion especially if there is abuse of any kind present. Up go the walls of protection of their inside emotions. They feel they are no longer allowed to express what is a natural emotion of fear and the individual, innocent soul of a child begins the journey of retreat rather than the joy of exploration!

Chapter 2
Who Have You Become

We are all aware, at this point in our development, that patterns do repeat themselves until someone chooses to break the cycle. That is why they say to look at your past and your family history because more times than not, you will see what direction you are headed and what you can become in the future. The scary part is we misread their choices and behaviors as our own because the onset of similar peer behaviors sometimes are latent and masked by what we want to see. When the behaviors do start to surface, we are already hooked into our illusions and we give others' illusions the benefit of being truth and ignore the red flags that start waving. We simply justify it away. No one is exempt from doing this to themselves or in relationships they have started. We become very tolerant human beings and say "...but I love this person, so I will do what it takes to fix that person" or "that is the way they are—I can't change them." The latter is correct, but that doesn't mean you sit there and take everything that is dished out to you if it means losing yourself and your self-esteem. If you don't know who you are then you will accept the abuse and continue in the cycle of a painful life. *Love does not mean pain!* Let us not get this confused with growth.

Love is found by experiencing lack of love. Wealth is found by experiencing poverty. Freedom is found by experiencing restriction. Happiness is found by experiencing sadness and depressions. Get the picture yet? Life is made up of opposites. It is what balances life. Growth is usually painful.

An example is the human body experiencing pain when our teeth start to break through as babies, but the change enables us to eventually eat different foods. If we feel emotional pain the system is the same. It allows us to experience new situations with a new light.

Many people believe crying is a sign of weakness, but that is incorrect. Crying is actually the first step to healing that specific situational emotion at the time. Cry, cry, cry...if it is difficult for you to cry, that means your protective walls are holding the flow of progress back like a dam. If you have built a really strong wall for yourself and the tears start to seep through the cracks, but you stop the flow, you had better take a reality check on exactly how much you have been suppressing behind that wall because the dam is about to break and some day it will! That is why the thought of "letting go" is so overwhelming and devastating because the years of suppression would create the feeling of being caught in a riptide with nowhere to grab.

This is when people begin to try and numb that which they are afraid to experience or relive. It becomes a "longing or hunger" that demands to be fed. People attempt to gratify these unfulfilled needs with physical consuming, such as food, drink, drugs, sex, alcohol, money and power. What this urge is impelling us toward is knowledge of self and improvement in the person's ability to gratify their personal desires. It impels us, but usually not in the right direction. The emotional effects take the form of an unconscious urging, instead, to eliminate relationships that inhibit personal growth. As "good ole boy" Socrates from long ago said, "To thine own self be true." The quest is to remember who we were before the *clutter* of fear and negative reinforcement was slowly dripped and conditioned into our psych and we became someone we don't even recognize at times.

Chapter 3
We Are Unique

We are all like snowflakes that fall from heaven. Each one is unique, each one is beautiful, each one is pure and free of all others until they hit the ground where they become the collective and create a whole new blanket that covers the ground. For a time that blanket is a sight of beauty, undisturbed, white and pure. That blanket creates a feeling of warmth, togetherness and security in an unspoken way and hushes the world for a moment at least. We stand back and wish we could hold on to that feeling of peacefulness. Alas, the world must continue and then begins the destruction of the untouched snow. This is cycle, a natural cycle, that will always return and always change the physical in some way until the next season begins a new cycle.

A baby is born. The baby is unique; he or she is pure and free of all others until it becomes a part of the collective. For a moment, this baby experiences freedom. The baby has no opinions, no insights, no values and no real ability to make choices. It is an empty computer ready to be programmed. It survives strictly by the senses of touch, smell, hearing, verbalization of needs through emotions and only emotions. There are no words yet, only the magnificent sensation of communication by emotion and "feeling". For a while, that is the only way we can communicate with a baby. We learn to read the needs and it is a universal education all humans experience.

When does it all start to change? When do we begin to punish a child for expressing emotions? When do we begin to tell a child that emotions are not to be expressed? When do we not acknowledge our feelings anymore? A child cannot create emotions as the emotions are programmed already into the system.

Resistance is created by not allowing a child, or any age range for that matter, to acknowledge their own feelings at the time they are feeling them. We begin to "train" the child to feel the way we do and if we are not feeling well, we send a distorted message. An example for clarity would be a child wanting a certain toy right now. We all know "now" means "now" to a child. As a trainer, we say "You don't want that now." The child says, "Yes, I do"!!! Now, how confusing is that to a child? They are saying how they feel and we are telling them they are not feeling that way. This begins the path of learning *not to be honest* with what we are feeling. We are taught that our emotions are nonexistent. So, where did they go? They hide out of fear of punishment or reprimand. That fear of rejection from the people who we look up to as role models becomes the focal point. But alas, the emotions are not gone! They are still inside of us waiting to be given permission to come out. The problem is that permission never comes and the emotions become suppressed even more as every day passes. We don't even know where they have gone! There is no outlet and a wall is created that becomes impossible to crack with no release portal available.

This brings us back to how we repress the *natural flow of* emotional process and the only thing left to take it's place is anger, frustration, hatred, depression and all the negative responses of resistance. We haven't come to understand yet that we need to feel the resistance to know what feels positive in the end if processed properly. We get so confused about what we are feeling because we are being forced to feel the way someone else feels. When we try to protect our own feeling about a situation, the elders usually out vote it. The elders do not usually help you process your feelings, they process based on what they know and expect. The end result is you begin to develop an esteem not your own.

How many times have you said "Now, how do I really feel about this situation?" You contemplate to the point of frustration and end up saying, "I don't know what I feel—I'm going to have a drink and think some more another day!" You begin to get angry, frustrated, depressed or just cry because you are so absent of your own emotions, more and more. You put the mask called "ego" on and wear it loudly, if necessary, to deter others from seeing that your *real self* has escaped you. It has been replaced with someone else's esteem and if you are to be accepted by them you had better not disagree with the one they gave you. It was surely given to you out of love! Please do not accept that thought!

I hate to say most of our esteem development is from ignorance of the elders who truly were doing the best they knew at the time, but were not yet so developed in their own esteem when they were training you. That is the cross we all have to bare, but that is also the blueprint for your journey in this life. It is not really a negative unless your attitude suggests otherwise, and, again, your attitude to change will be learned from those same elders as well. If they have a negative attitude, you may follow with the same unchanging viewpoint.

Here we go on that *cycle thing*. They can't possibly allow you to have an emotion that is unacceptable to them. *We were taught this way and look how we turned out.* Ouch! Adults better take a reality check of self before something is said to a child because a child can spot more than we think. Remember, their mind isn't so full of clutter yet they can't see what is real. They may fight back and usually do until submissiveness reigns. Make sure children aren't the mirror to your flaws.

Emotions are good and as we will discuss later, balance is the key, not elimination. A person does not have free reign to act on the emotions if that emotion is harm to herself/himself or others. This is where boundaries and limits come in to play.

Chapter 4
Limits and Boundaries

What exactly do we mean by limits and boundaries? It could simply mean the difference of saying "yes" or "no." It is difficult to set boundaries for ourselves if we do not know who we are and what we stand for individually. Yes, our teachers, parents or the peers we are told to respect, have taught us limits and boundaries. When we are young, we are impressionable. We believe we are being guided correctly by their words and yet the example is usually opposite of the words. More confusion? The question to ask is from what level of awareness are we learning? Obviously we don't know that when we are young. We have to entrust what is being said as true. Hence the onslaught of future anger when we find out that "What I say and what I do" do not always correspond even though it is expected for us to know which one is right if they conflict. We are searching for the right answers, so we begin an unknown path to find something, which already resides in us. This is where the frustration and resistance initializes into the picture.

Reuniting with your own truth is your power and your peace. Overcoming the inappropriate boundaries and limitations set up for you by others cause the conflict inside you. Re-creating new boundaries for yourself that will keep you happy and secure is a lot easier said than done. Right? We have spent all of our years trusting we were on the right path only to find out later by the ones that trained us that we messed up. What is a person to do? Do you get the feeling that we spend most of our time confused? You are right! That is why it is so very important that you start the journey to finding out who you are underneath the build up of clutter. Believe it or not, you are under there somewhere!

Life on the earth plane is merely the schoolroom and your homework is to sort through the myriad of obstacles set in front of you to help you find the peace you seek. Yourself. Remember the section on opposites of life? You have experienced what is wrong for you when something isn't working and you know how that feels, so when you find what is right for you, you will release the frustration and angers. You will know because you will feel at peace. If you accept life as others have ordained for you, you will never feel the joy of finding yourself and the happiness it brings automatically. You will continue to feel the anger and frustrations of a resistance put upon you by others. Oneness with yourself and reuniting with the God in you is your goal. You may feel God has forsaken you, but maybe he feels he has been forsaken. He is there waiting to be rediscovered! No one said school was ever easy. At birth, you are in the "Kindergarten of life." It is time to be reborn and I am not talking about a religious faction. Know yourself above all else.

All things change. Do not ever feel you have to give permanent reality to things that are always temporary. Everything is constantly shifting to shed the old and allow the new to emerge. The biggest problem is resistance to a natural process. When you are in emotional pain, ask yourself what you need to shed or change in your life? What part of your identity is being attacked or resistant? Do you want to take this over in school of life again or learn it now? You know by now you don't get promoted to the next level without passing the test. You will know you have passed the test because you will say and you will feel strongly. "I know, I know." No one will be able to put doubt in your head or sway your feelings or intellect regarding that specific situation.

If you are still doubtful, fearful, protective of your own opinion, then I guarantee you have not quite satisfied yourself that you have found another piece of yourself. When you feel at peace and your behavior automatically changes to mirror what you know, you have broken a cycle. That will be the arms of God lifting you up to the next level.

Now you can set a healthy, clear and firm boundary for yourself for the particular situation that you just became enlightened. No one can step over it, step on it, kick or spit on it because "you know you know". You can maintain a peace inside as they attempt to prove you wrong. And believe me; they will give it their best shot.

I remember one of the times I was down and out, no money and stuck at home; a friend of mine told me I couldn't go to a party because I couldn't afford to participate financially. What a friend, heh? Kick you when you are down enough on yourself. I had enough esteem left to extricate him out of my life. If I had no self esteem, I probably would have whimpered and cried in my room and waited for the next kick to really feel as bad as I felt I deserved.

Letting others sabotage us and cross over boundaries that are weak to begin with or weakened is unhealthy, but not even as much as we sabotage ourselves by doing excess of drugs, alcohol, food and sex, to name a few, which weakens our boundaries of rational thinking. It is all learned behavior or, in some cases, behavior not yet learned. Learned behavior can be changed if you are aware of what needs to change, are willing to take the chance that God will help you make the changes and if there is honest effort and commitment on your part. Would you learn to ride a bike if someone else did the driving all the time? Your limits and boundaries will always be tested, so the stronger you become in belief of yourself and what makes you happy and secure, the less the testing will affect you and the less other people will be able to affect your emotional well being. You will not be dependent on the externals of life, which may guide you down an incorrect path.

Chapter 5
Unhealthy Boundaries

People need to have some limitation or you would be acting out your feelings, which you know can get intense at times. You can be angry with someone, scream harsh words to them and even think thoughts that might not be appropriate. That is feeling. That is yours. No one can take these thoughts away from you. You can only try to help guide yourself through the thoughts to a point of understanding which help you regain your emotional balance. You do need to understand and evaluate where the thoughts are originating. Are they all things you mean or are you insecure that your safety and happiness is being threatened? It could be either one, but you ultimately need to accept the responsibility and consequences of any action you might take by acting out your feelings in a physical manner.

This is where parents need to take the time to seek out the actual cause of the feelings for children and you need to be aware yourself to do it effectively. It is not really learning to process if you react to the behavior rather than trying to teach the child to find the actual cause. How many times do we hear, "I don't know what is wrong," or the response is totally different than the cause. Do not answer for the child. Ask the child questions and let them answer for themselves. Let them learn to think for themselves.

Parents have a tendency at times to liberate a child from taking responsibility or consequences and don't follow through with their own laws. What does that message relate? Parents may have poor boundaries themselves and are afraid their own child will not like them. Children grow up to ages of maturity still wanting approval from their parents, to the detriment of the child at times, so don't worry about the child not liking you. The need for parental approval is strong and lasting even in the worst of cases.

In fact, it will have the opposite effect where the child will feel you don't care. Maintain balance. No extremes, please. We need to teach a lesson and not abuse them into a state of fear and isolation. How many times is a child punished, and most of the time they don't even know why? "Because I said so..." Okay, parents, nice try, but let us not take the easy way out on the one thing that is the most important thing in your life. *Your children.*

How many times have I heard this? "I would give my life for this child..." but dare take the time to teach now, when you have more important things to do. I guess you don't need to explain your actions, because you are the boss. Maybe you don't have an answer because it was never explained to you. You never got processed. Oh, that cycle again! Ignorance breeds ignorance. What a future we have before us. "Do as I say and not as I do..."

Does confusion seem to be more clearly a part of our education? Let me see, where did I read that the best teacher taught through example. I think it was a very old book, so it is not a new problem. Cycles, again. Let us take a good and honest look at ourselves and admit we may just not know the answers all the time and quit trying to pretend that we are the perfect role models. We are creating carbon copies of confusion. A child just needs to know she/he is loved and setting healthy limits and boundaries that do not suffocate their creativity is part of the process.

The unhealthy boundaries created or boundaries never created at all are usual in dysfunctional families. They have a problem setting boundaries to ensure safety and security in the home because life is mostly chaos. There is no time for process. It is strictly reactionary and in survival stages of getting the basic needs met of everyone involved.

A boundary is to take care of you and your esteem. It does not mean abandonment. If someone does abandon you, it may not be their choice or it could be they were manipulating you through control. They possibly stepped over your boundary without respect to why a boundary is even there. They are not respecting your feelings of safety and security as to where they stop and you begin. Being inconsistent with setting firm and clear boundaries creates anxiety for all the people involved.

How many people have heard, "It's my way or the highway," does this sound like someone who respects you and your sense of well-being? Then you begin thinking, gee, I guess I don't exist. There must be something wrong with me. So, they do leave you or abuse you to the point that you wish them harm or harm to yourself. And if you have not had healthy training in setting or accepting good boundaries, then you have more tendencies to act out your feelings. This results in consequences of jail, hospital, or the "streets," where you could become that which you are feeling. Lost. Now that is real. No one is going to touch your feelings now because you have none. Maybe that is your new beginning. The computer is about as empty as it could be. It has crashed. So you get a new hard drive and start filling it up with what you want in life. You just need to figure out what you want to program into your personal computer. You have plenty of time now. No one will bother you. They think you are gone.

Obviously, I am being somewhat facetious, but the point is the same. When you feel the most lost is when you have emptied the old "crap" out of you. You automatically start searching to get it all back, but the past has outlived its usefulness. It doesn't work anymore. You are free. Let go now. Live your life. Now you can follow *your path* because you aren't impressed by the opinions of others anymore.

SIGNS OF UNHEALTHY BOUNDARIES

- **Self abuse. Sexual and physical abuse. Food Abuse.**
- **Expecting others to take care of you.**
- **Letting other people tell you who you are and what you like.**
- **Letting other people control you.**
- **Feeling as if your choices are minimal to none.**
- **Assuming others know what you want.**
- **Allowing people to drain the life out of you.**
- **Giving as much as you can for approval.**
- **Not knowing what your boundaries are...**
- **Allowing someone to be inappropriate with you verbally or physically.**
- **Not standing up for what you believe in.**
- **Allow someone to speak for you.**
- **Doing for others and not for yourself.**
- **Spilling your guts with someone new.**
- **Talking and not listening.**
- **Stepping inside someone's comfort zone before you are invited.**

God gave us a gift of choice as with no other living being on earth. Boundaries are guidelines for us to remain safe with who we are becoming. Choices allow us to be flexible and to change with the circumstances.

Chapter 6
Setting Boundaries

I have been asked many times, "What choices do we have as children? We have to do what our parents tell us. How can we maintain a positive attitude when we are being abused and there is no place to escape except to the streets?"

I would say these are reasons gangs, cults and surrogate "families" are created. This is why children start early with drugs and alcohol because someone has been able to persuade them it is the cool path. All they know is that they are not being listened to at home. So, if they can escape to a perceived better place, physically or mentally, with a person of a "desirable" life-style or someone who appears *to understand and make it all better*, the choice is obvious. Someone is taking an interest whether good or bad. It is difficult to see the wrongdoer in this.

Children actually have greater sources now days to get help. They didn't have as many avenues several years ago for the children who were being abused and are now parents. These parents are struggling themselves to overcome their past demons and their children are feeling the brunt. It is no one's fault. We do with what we know at the time. Know there is another way. There is no need to keep fighting the unknown. Accept a helping hand.

Parents, do you have an answer for your children who know nothing about self-esteem and self respect because they are struggling just to exist? I place the responsibility of these questions back in your hands. You have made a choice to have children and now you have a choice on how to raise them. Look into their eyes. Do your see yourself in them? Try helping them by getting help. It is okay to need and seek help sometimes. Don't expect the children are the only ones that need the help.

I find it rather interesting many people are placing responsibility of teaching appropriate behavior of the child on the school system, jails and the judicial system and then the parents do not back up the system. They remain in denial of where the problems originated. It takes mutual effort to smooth out communications after so much damage has been done. It is not impossible. The attitude needs to change to nurture the new growth, not allow the old behaviors to resurface and repeat the cycles, again. This makes it difficult for the teachers who really do care because their hands are tied. Where are the parents?

I knew a friend who had a child of teenage years. This parent went out to a party almost every night and left the child at home. The child got very upset and scared one night and called me because the child knew where I would be and how to get a hold of me. She couldn't reach her mother. The mother used to wonder why the child was so depressed and despondent most of the time. The child counted on me for the security and stability because she always knew where I would be at any given time. Children need to know they are secure and safe. Even if there are problems, they can accept them if they know that they are loved and they are part of a unit.

Parents! Wake up! Wake up! Wake Up! Quit pointing the finger somewhere else. Your child wants to please you and all children are praying for some boundaries and limitations! They need to know you care through the guidance you give them. Knowing what unhealthy boundaries are will help you see what is sabotaging everyone's happiness.

The children have been stripped of their feelings and now you won't listen to what is really being said by misunderstanding their activities and behavior. Remember, you have taught them to suppress their emotions, so they go to the only other avenue left to them and that is through their behavior. They are acting out what they are feeling. They may be struggling with any concept that says life is beautiful. If you can't see the beauty, how can you expect them to see it? Do not punish them for your lack of awareness of taking responsibility to change, grow, and learn.

Don't make the mistake thinking a family is automatically dysfunctional if the parents are not together. I have seen very healthy and happy children progress nicely with the separation of parents. In fact, one instance was a blessing. The pressure eased up and the children were able to breathe more easily. They learn it can be better for two people to go in separate directions and create a better life for the children in the long run. The fighting and conflict resolved itself. The greater lesson was to stand for what you believe to be right and that one doesn't have to live in dysfunction by settling for less than a truly loving home. There may need to be sacrifices in the beginning, but it can be worth more in the end. This isn't always the case, as bitterness can be an evil dagger for all. The parents need to make an effort to assure the child the breakup has nothing to do with them. Do not pull the child into the middle of a chaotic situation that is not their issue.

Everyone makes mistakes and that is okay. We can admit them and go on. Making mistakes helps us to set the boundaries necessary for us to be safe the next time around. Mistakes help us to be more clear and firm in developing the boundaries.

If we, as a people, don't turn this negative reinforcement around, this planet will digress backwards until we are controlled by the negative. We could be led into pseudo "loving arms" like the "Jimmy Jones group" who were very basically led to their death because they allowed someone else to think and speak for them. They gave what was left of themselves away.

If you are the child, you can take the first step. See a counselor at school or a teacher you trust and feel comfortable with who has understanding and compassion. Let them help guide you to your next step. If you are an adult, do the same. Find someone you trust to help you find the next step for you. It is all about helping each other to achieve a happy outcome.

If gangs could take their anger and turn it into encouraging energy, what a positive influence they could have on youth. They have the concepts of loyalty and trust and camaraderie down, but the anger is in the way and their boundaries are distorted because of what they are trying to forget.

Why do many people fail to set healthy boundaries? Some people don't even realize there is such a thing as a personal boundary. We have laws that protect us, guide us to stay focused and orderly, but emotional boundaries are overlooked and only can be monitored by the individual. The government cannot oversee what is on the inside of every individual. Your best friend can't even read your mind. So, that leaves it up to you.

To reiterate, you need to find out what is inside you or what is hidden in you. Boundaries can be established by trial and error of life experiences. Peers can teach it or watching others we would like to emulate is always available. Hopefully, the role model is positive, but sometimes we do not know this until we are standing in front of a judge.

When you do not know how you think and feel, you cannot possibly set boundaries that keep you safe or secure. You become the slave to the boundaries of others, which is not a fun place to be at times. This is when fear, anger, frustration, impatience, friction, suspicion and prejudice can keep you on that lower plain of existence. How many times have you let someone speak for you or make decisions for you? You quietly sit there and say to yourself "That isn't what I want..."

The fear of rejection or abandonment is too great and is the most principal aspect for you right now. You might even think to yourself this person must be in control, because he/she can set boundaries so easily! Wrong! If that person needs to control you they are not in control of themselves. The more control that is exerted on you, the less control they have of themselves. These people have a need to control something, so who is the easy target? The one who lets themselves be controlled. Both have poor boundaries.

❧

Chapter 7
Fear and Anger

Having poor boundaries cause us to take many forms of deceptive behaviors that mask strength and control. For example the "big ego" is a deception. Those are the people with the lowest self-esteem. In other words, the louder they yell or the angrier they get, you can bet they are "masking". What are they masking? Fear and hurt. The two go hand in hand.

Before anger, there is always a fear factor that has been touched and the anger comes out to protect the fear or deep hurt. They have not resolved the issue from their past because the sting is still there. Next time someone gets angry with you, ask them, "What is it you are afraid of happening?" They will probably avoid the comment or not really know the honest answer right away. They may continue to yell, but I would bet in the privacy of their own thoughts, they may ponder that very question. They may never admit it and that is a shame because they are inhibiting any more growth of the relationship. They are comfortable being impatient, angry, frustrated, suspicious, prejudiced and any person who is lost and needy will become a target. The insecure person will not have the esteem to stand up to them. Intimidation is the worst kind of abuse and being fearful of that is just as bad.

Fear is disbelieving in yourself and anger protects that disbelief in yourself. If you cannot express anger in healthy directions or at all, you cannot protect yourself in a safe and secure space. Anger is an emotion that needs to be owned by everyone but understanding it and controlling its force and purpose is a skill. Skills are learned.

People fear humiliation. They don't like being wrong; they also fear truth and love. The three biggest fears are being taken advantage of, rejection and abandonment and fear of the unknown. We fear to set boundaries for fear of losing something or someone. Have you given any thought that maybe the thing or the person might be worth losing if it is causing you pain and upsetting your safety and security? It certainly would make sense that if it is causing you anguish, pain or distress, maybe it is time to look for another road. If someone is not respecting your boundary, then maybe they do not really respect you. Realistically, would you say that is love? I think not.

You need to start challenging your fears and ask yourself what it means. Fear is only as strong as your need to run from it. The greater the need to avoid it, the more control it has on you. Remember I talked about balancing yourself. Sometimes the pendulum needs to swing in the opposite direction completely in order to balance in the middle again. It will always feel awkward and uncomfortable to start something new. The first day of school is awkward until you get settled in.

Master magicians of the world who create an illusion that keeps you from living the life you deserve use fear. They thrive on creating fear and intimidating sensations in others because they themselves are so scared that if backed into a corner by someone stronger they would probably fight, fold or take flight. They may never admit on their own that they might be more vulnerable than one would think because of the "ego mask."

The person who can openly express anger with the strength to stand up for their belief does feel safe to talk directly about an issue because it may be in a safe and validating environment. The problems arise when people have been conditioned in the invalidating environments, which have been induced, by fear, intimidation, physical/mental abuse and hostility. They either turn on themselves or on someone else when the anger erupts.

If children or adults use an indirect route of venting their anger and hostility, they obviously have been conditioned that expressing anger is unsafe or unacceptable. They turn to drugs, alcohol and self-mutilation as a way to avoid involvement and direct conflict with others. They do not feel safe confronting the conflicts. Too much pain is involved from their conditioning and experience. They sabotage their happiness and possible intimate relationships because they cannot express they are fearful.

To pull all of these concepts together for you to this point: Know *your* beliefs, know what *you* think and feel and determine who and how others can affect you and when. If you fear losing something or someone which is not part of your own true essence and allowing others to create your boundaries and/or cross over your boundaries, you have created an unsafe insecure environment for yourself and your family. You know you have now misplaced your self-respect, self worth and very possibly, your life. It doesn't have to be this way. EVER! Start paying attention and listen to your own body for the answers, for it will tell you what is right or wrong for you. It is the best friend you have and was created by God for your own protection. Pay attention to the level of your emotions because this too will help you gauge the resistance from the other players.

For every action, there is an equal and opposite reaction. This is a very simple equation we have all heard and it works in many areas of life. It could also be said "to the degree something is missing is the degree which you will search for it." If you missed a lot of love growing up, you will seek it out in an equal degree of searching, which can become neediness if a vast hole exists. How love was defined to you will be the method by which you seek it. If you thought love was being abused, you will seek out abuse as love. You have nothing else to measure it by. Love in its purest form will cross your path one day, you will recognize it, but will you strive to understand it and allow it to change you?

Chapter 8
Tools of Success

God has given us all of the tools to make a success of our lives. Defining what success is for us needs to be a unique and personal gauge. Somehow it gets lost in the myriad of clutter that has entered through the opinions and judgments of others. People become involved in jobs that were the dreams of their parents and end up resenting life and the parents because they feel it is too late to start over. How many of you ever said, I always wanted to be this or do that, but..." The excuses come flying from all directions. The negative reinforcement received from the people we desire to respect us are usually the ones to shoot our ideas and dreams right to the ground. Some of the responses might be; "You can't make any money doing that, your grades aren't good enough, you need money and you don't have it." I hope you have heard enough success stories on TV to know that those are limitations and fears of someone else.

There have been studies that reveal the majority of self-made millionaires have not even a high school education! What do these people have that we did not find in all of the schooling that we got? They are skilled at life and they have a high self-esteem, which was taught and nurtured with their life experience. They learned the hard way and took risks that broke through the limitations put upon them by others. It is all learned. They believed in themselves and had the burning desire to have more. They found the one part of their essence, which was their unique gift or talent and used it. It may have been from desperation and being backed into a corner or simply a "whim" of chance. What did they have to lose from their perspective? They were used to having nothing so what makes the difference if they take the chance? They survived being poor, so they can do that again if they failed. They also had a clear head on their shoulders. They did not sabotage their success by drinking or drugging themselves into an escape delirium. They started one step at a time with an idea. An idea costs nothing.

There are some basic realities of human behavior, which I believe these millionaires had to have to proceed forward. I am not suggesting everyone try to achieve this status as this may not be what your individual success story is to read. Your story could simply be having a healthy relationship or finding your niche that is your comfort level. The goal is to find what satisfies you and makes your happy! You will attract the people to you who will accept you for who you are. Let them find their own space. Take an inventory of your present friends and your environment. It will be a mirror of what you are accepting for yourself. It is a fact. I am not talking about images and money because those can be facades of what is behind them. I am talking about the dignity, self worth and self-respect that surround you. You "know" when you are around someone who is at peace with themselves because you can feel it. They do not have to display it and they are not condescending in any way towards those who are not there yet.

High esteemed people have comfortable boundaries, which they will acknowledge to you in a non-threatening manner and maintain respect for yours without having to probe you. I suppose you could say this is proper etiquette for respecting the feelings and actions of others and let them grow at their own speed. Low esteemed are not giving and only are "taking" from others. High esteemed people will simply and quietly excuse themselves from the situation altogether. You cannot respect other people's boundaries and feelings if you don't have the same respect for yourself. If you have an empty cup, you will be searching for someone with a full cup to fill yours. In time, you will deplete their cup and they will have to leave you to replenish their cup.

When they do leave, your cup empties out because the contents were not yours to begin with-and there you sit again. Depleted, empty, lost and depressed. You will hear me say this in every book I write. It deserves to be understood and repeated. Who have you turned back to again? You! Do you still not like what you see? Now if you are tired of being depleted and confused and ready to look at the true reality, your reality, not someone else's reality, then you might want to shelve your present beliefs and assumptions of the past and take a look at the natural and truthful realities of human behavior.

Your tools for success are all compacted into a physical container called a body. You have the physical aspects of the body, which help with physical tasks to be completed. Everyone is aware of their body even if some have a distorted view. If any of the physical parts are taken away or not working the body adjusts itself to function in a new way.

You have the mental aspects, which control the physical. Physical does not function without the mental. Therefore, it would seem that the mental part would be the part to focus on first. What affects the mental will ultimately affect the physical, as we will discuss later. Let us focus on your new mental and emotional realities. The physical will follow right along.

Chapter 9
Natural Truths

There are two paths to take regarding the first truth. All responsibilities and consequences which affect you directly are your own decisions and choices.

There is a path of benefit and a path of suffering. Sometimes, we have to take the path of suffering to understand the path to benefit. Hopefully, we learn from the path of suffering and don't get comfortable there. You will be beat up at an early age, if you do not learn to be in charge of your own life. Who is making your decisions? Who is allowing others to be in charge of your life? Denying your own needs is destructive to your self-esteem. It leaves you vulnerable to others 'opinions, attitudes, demands and expectations. It requires you to agree with others and need their approval and acceptance.

This is a stage that is difficult for the adolescent because they are bound by this constant need for approval and acceptance. That is their natural stage of development. The parents who cannot fill their own cup will deprive the child of any knowledge and appreciation of life and cause the child to seek out something they don't even recognize exists for the rest of their lives. Hopefully the child learns he/she can find and create fulfillment for themselves. This is when adolescents feel they are at the mercy of the establishment, the law, the parents and life in general because they are caught up in negative and invalidating environments that continue to feed their fears and doubts. The more fearful they are, the farther they run away.

How you are is the example you are setting for someone who may be looking to you for answers. Know the outcome you wish before you start. Decide what you can do to make the most of your situation and maintain your positive attitude.

You can do anything within your perceived capabilities. You still take responsibility for how you do it. Do you ever feel trapped? How many times have you done something that you didn't want to do? Was there a price to pay? Was there benefit or suffering? You should not ever feel guilty for your mistakes, defeats or failures. Putting blame and guilt on yourself or someone else is totally unjustified because you are only acting within your present knowledge capability at the time of the action. Maybe you need more information or different information to increase your capabilities and insight comes when you are sick and tired of being *sick and tired*. There is always a next time with new information. Your capabilities depend on you and your willingness to be open to new directions, attitudes and beliefs in yourself. If you limit yourself by crystallizing your intelligence, so you cannot achieve anymore, then you won't. That simple. Listening to others giving you input that is negative doesn't help because you absorb it and say "what is the use?"

Remember, the other people may not be speaking from an informed level of capability either. Just because your neighbor says he will teach you to play tennis, doesn't mean he will do it well. If you want to be good at something, find someone that is good in that area and ask them for guidance. The majority of people would love to help if they see enthusiasm. I do not need approval from anyone as I am learning something new for myself. Unknown paths can be more interesting. The point is expanding your capabilities, be the best you can and understand that you pay a big price for uninformed choices. Think twice and make a more informed decision next time. *You do exist and that is important because YOU are unique.*

If you feel you have to prove your worth and importance by good behavior and accomplishments, then someone is sending you a message that you are unworthy. When you have high self-esteem, you will not have a need to be validated because you will know you were doing what you prefer to do rather than what you prefer not to do. It was your choice and you accept your choice because it was your choice. If you seek approval, check your cup for its level of needs.

If you look externally to exist, you will remain depressed. Comparing yourself to others is unjustified as a measure of your worth and existence: as you are unique! Have you forgotten that already? You can only take care of the dominating and/or conflicting needs that get in the way of the desire to do better. *The conflicting needs* usually originate from another who has a different view. Again, functioning from their desires, not yours, creates conflict on the inside. You were created to be you.

Guilt is the most destructive emotion. You need not ever condemn or be condemned for what you do. This is a big issue! Guilt creates intense emotional turmoil and feelings of unworthiness, which constrict constructive activity. Are you to blame? NO! Are you responsible? YES! Could you have done better? That depends on your awareness. Your awareness is how clearly you see and understand that which affects your life. Let people make their own mistakes and live their own lives and the guilt will melt right away. Only if it is a matter of life and death, do you intervene. Guilt has been and is used to manipulate.

Making someone feel they have to provide or else they will be condemned to guilt wastes a lot of precious time. Be happy with your choice even if it is wrong. You will learn from it and move on to the next situation. Just say, "Oh well, what's next?" Keep moving ahead. *Do not intervene with a person's choice or allow someone to intervene in your choices unless it is life or death. By all means, life is valuable and it would be the correct thing to step in, even though you are not responsible for their outcomes. Otherwise, guide them by allowing them to experience their decisions.*

When you are young, you have minimal awareness of life. If you were overly protected it usually is because your parents didn't want you to have to experience the consequences. This is a mistake. You don't learn this way. Parents are limiting your chances to increase your awareness pool and you will eventually have to experience situations when you get older with much greater consequences.

I can't count the number of issues I had to learn later in life because my parents limited my choices while growing up. It was painful and expensive for me. They felt they knew the outcomes, so they thought they were saving me time and anguish by protecting me from the horrible conclusions. Alas, the opposite occurred. I not only experienced it all anyway, but it cost me more in the end when I did.

Let your children experience their choices at a younger age when the expense is only a feeling, so they can deal with the consequences under a guiding and friendly hand of understanding. They certainly do not need to hear, "We told you so." Who are you trying to impress that you are right? *You are without fault.*

If you feel you are always at fault and always making mistakes, then there must be something wrong with you. Incorrect! There is only something wrong with your awareness. You may have heard God does not make mistakes or trash. When you allow others to think for you, make your decisions, tell you how to dress, you open yourself up to be vulnerable to faults and mistakes. It is only a mistake if you do what someone else feels you should be doing. Isn't this a form of control? This is not to say you cannot ask someone for help if you would like to dress a different way, act a different way, or feel a different way. That still makes it your choice for what you want at the time. One of the gifts God gave you is the power of choice. When that is taken away, you lose your freedom. You can make mistakes and take the wrong paths by choice just to see where it takes you. You will learn from it and hopefully return to the original path with a new awareness. No one needs to judge you. You do enough of that to yourself.

Believe me, I feel comfortable saying that everyone else could look in the mirror and make a few mind boggling realizations that they are not so perfect! The only difference is they have learned to cover up their mistakes. If you make the effort to do the right thing and have the faith that you are where you are supposed to be at the time, whatever the situation, God will pull you through the rest of the way once the lesson is learned. If you give up and start playing those old tapes "I am no good," you will fall prey to the pity pot of life.

Feeling good mentally, physically and spiritually is your right.

Are you settling for less in these areas? We have all done this at some point. It is your choice to stay in the lesser state or take baby steps to find the balance for yourself. I am sure everyone can find one situation where they had a glimpse of the perfect state of balance. I know those who have been abused will probably say they can't think of one time, but dig deeply. Think of one person, situation or thing that you experienced that made you yearn for that *perfect state*. It only takes a glimpse to give you a direction. "Feeling good" is natural, but people using false stimulants to achieve or maintain a high are not natural. They are creating a false state, which creates negative results in the long run. There are no "strong" or "weak" people, only people who have a different intensity to motivations created by their awareness to date. Change your awareness and you change your motivation.

Your purpose has meaning only to you.

It is known, by this time, that if you do not love yourself, you cannot truly love another. Everything has a purpose and makes a contribution to life. Making mistakes even contributes to your ultimate purpose. Other people can learn from your mistakes and you from their mistakes. The key is "learning." Learning expands your awareness and an expanded awareness creates more freedom with less stress to make wiser decisions. Isn't it good feeling when you can say, "I learned that the hard way!" You can enjoy the feeling that you do not have to relive that experience, unless of course you choose, and go on to the next experience one step higher than you were before. If you fall down some steps, you can still go back up the ladder a different way or a different speed. You know you know.

Everyone is not at the same level of learning and they may not be ready to take the same steps. They may need to take different steps to achieve their unique goals. Do not push your goals on to them. Everyone will intuitively feel if the path is right for them. If you know yourself better than they do, they cannot control your path. I may sound repetitive about increasing your awareness about life, but no two people have the same awareness. That is what makes us unique. So why think you need to follow the same path of another? Our awareness is constantly changing. Every time we make a decision, we change our awareness. Every time we learn something, we change our awareness. You are a different person every morning you wake up. If you stay limited and think limiting thoughts, your awareness will not expand and your feelings and motivations will not change. Distorted thoughts create distorted actions and reactions. Positive thoughts create positive actions and reactions. We have been conditioned with more of the distorted areas as human beings because that sells.

If gangs were created out of dysfunction to develop a "family" of loyalty, caring and camaraderie in a safe, secure and validating environment for its members, changing their attitudes and reasons about their existence to a positive existence rather than continue the destruct mode they came from would be a powerful energy mankind could use.

Children who rise above mistakes of the parents and become the example is so possible because children have less clutter to manifest damaging behaviors from layers of negative suppressions. They can bounce back faster than adults. Their philosophy of togetherness, loyalty and honor are wonderful and insightful, but it is the attitude they have learned that is destructive and is destroying that which God created for us to enjoy.

Who will be the first to take the challenge? Who will lead the children to the victories of peace? You have the power to make the changes. How many children wish they could go home, live in peace, eat at the dinner table with their family and enjoy the security of the home? We have lost this somewhere along the line.

Chapter 10
Value Judging

There are three reasons for our "feel bad" behavior. The most common is resisting ourselves and justifying our actions. We identify ourselves through those actions. We condemn ourselves for not doing what we "should" do based on the values and beliefs of others. The second is resisting others for their actions that do not conform to our values and beliefs. The third is to resist an unwanted situation, condition or event. All are forms of value judging. What is value judging?

Value judging is criticizing, condemning, blaming or finding fault with someone because their behavior doesn't conform to our values and beliefs. Value judging is destructive. How can we judge a person when they are only doing what their present awareness allows? Children blame their parents for their problems and yes, the parents need to take responsibility for what they have taught and the example they have set. However, they too, were only doing what their awareness permitted them to do at the time. This works in reverse as well. The parents cannot point the finger at the children for the same reason. It is so easy to point the finger at the other person because many people have not been taught to take responsibility for their own actions.

The reality is the responsibility of the decision you make falls on your shoulders and you suffer the consequences. When you make a bad choice either on your own or at the prompting of someone else, where are they when the ax falls? Usually, they are somewhere else. All fingers point back to you, so why don't you take control of what you have control over and that is, your own actions. The satisfaction for this is immense. If you still feel the world has control over you and there is just no way out of your plight, ask yourself what you have, at this very point in time, that you do have control over.

This may sound simplistic, but it gives you a beginning. You have control over what color to make your hair, the thoughts that go through your mind, the people you have in your life as examples. Everyone has various things they can control no matter how small. If you are an adolescent in an abusive environment, you may not have control over your family's behavior and actions, but you do have control in finding someone you trust to help you find the right path so you can live a productive and happy life. Do not feel you are betraying your family. It is your right to have the chance at happiness. I truly believe that people know when something is not right, but they feel trapped and loyal to the ones they are supposed to be respecting despite the dysfunction. If you can find a small portion of strength to find someone you trust or simply pray that God brings you the right person, it will be done.

You need others in time of pain and trouble, but you need to recognize that when you are vulnerable, some people will kick you when you are down, take advantage of you and make attempts to make you feel guilty or dependent. This is how they keep control of you. Choosing the people who support you is not always easy to manifest unless you become astute at what makes your decisions feel right for you. If you have no esteem of faith left, it can be the worst feeling ever. Just remember that whoever is creating those "bad vibes" has a low or lower esteem than you may be experiencing. Get away from them. Tell yourself, "I don't need this right now or ever if that is what it takes." "I am only temporarily down and if you are not going to support me, your history in my book." A higher esteemed person will guide you, not tear you down.

You can bet I follow that mantra because I refuse to let anyone cause me undue pain and anguish. As soon as I start to feel negativity, manipulation or control surrounding my essence, I nip it in the bud quickly. I always say, don't take my kindness, generosity and softness as a weakness where you feel you can chip away at my esteem little by little. You will see a phoenix rise up from the ground and put you in a place you didn't expect very quickly.

It's best not to interfere in someone else's decision unless their life depends on it. This is a concept very difficult to maintain. We always want to give input even when not asked. It is best to ask questions and make them answer through their own thoughts. Decisions are a belief and tension is caused by conflict of many people's beliefs. If your own beliefs are not firm in your own mind, the conflict of others' viewpoints will keep you off balance. If the latter is the case and you can't make up your own mind, this is the moment when other people start telling you what you should be doing and this is where you start to lose your control. Value judging starts to seep through the cracks and you begin to believe the external input rather than your own insights.

There is a simple exercise for making decisions even if your intuition is not working very well at the time. Let us say you have a decision to make. You state the question out loud to yourself or write it down. Then write down the different possibilities you feel are justifiable. Start with the first possibility and state "if I make the decision to go this way, will it give me a feeling of strength and freedom or a feeling of weakness and conflict?" If you listen to your body, it will give you the answer.

Go to the next possibility and do the same process. Try this with decisions that you already know the answer and see how your body reacts. As you become more comfortable with this process, the larger decisions will become easier to make and the decision making process will become faster. A feeling of confidence will start to make its way back into your life. The biggest hurdle is not listening to others. Really pay attention to how your body reacts to each possibility. If the answer is the less desired answer, your body will get tense, your brow may furrow or you simply get a bad taste in your mouth. If the answer is the correct one, your body will feel free and flowing. You may even say "Yes, this sounds/feels right!" If you are still confused, that is all right. Confusion is sometimes saying it is not right for a decision to be made right now. Do not let anyone force you to make a decision you are not ready to make because it usually ends up being the wrong direction for you. If they need an answer right now, follow what your body tells you. If it feels right, take a risk. If it feels wrong, back out.

I have found when I agree to something my body resists, I usually kick myself later. That doubt gets me in trouble every time. Hopefully, the consequences aren't too bad and the lesson is learned. The higher your self-esteem, the more sure you are of trusting your own intuition or inner knower. It has all of the answers. It has only benefit in mind for you and you alone.

You see, value judging is inappropriate and destructive. Comparing two people's performance, criticizing, praising or putting a time on a compliment are all destructive. Everyone marches to a different drummer and each needs to be considered as a unique individual with unique talents, gifts and contributions to society. There are no strengths or weaknesses, only developed and undeveloped areas. Everything is learned and with effort and practice, like in a sport, you become the expert of your own life. Discipline and flexibility equals' freedom and increasing your awareness helps you focus your disciplines. The change is awkward at first and gradual. What your mind considers, it believes, and in turn, the mind does. What your mind doesn't consider anymore, it dismisses. Hopefully you will be dismissing any form of value judging of yourself and others. Tend to your life and fertilize your own garden. When you are in a position of plenty, you can give back to others. This time your cup is full and you have taken care of your needs, so you do not need to take from others.

༄

Chapter 11
Perceptions

As I stated earlier in the book, we are all searching for one common goal and that is love. We want to be loved and to look in the mirror and love what we see in ourselves. We want to share love with someone. We create the obstacles to loving others or being loved by others because we fear punishment, pain, abandonment or rejection. Fear as I have mentioned, is merely a lack of awareness and knowledge of the possible unknown. We have the choice of remaining in the dark and being fearful by running to drugs, alcohol, promiscuity, gambling or whatever the addiction of choice might be. You are just diverting your attentions from dealing with the real or imagined problems. Both perceptions are valid, of course, because it feels real to us.

Let us take a look at some possible areas that we could use enlightenment and increase our awareness of what we do to create obstacles to growth and loving. People can alter their lives by altering attitudes You are what you think. You probably have heard this before. The response is usually the same "How can I change my attitude if everything and everyone around me is negative?"

What have you learned already? You and you alone are responsible for your actions and your results. If you do not have the power because of age, find someone who does. This means you may need to shed some old behavior yourself, shed some friends or shed an environment that is pure negativity.

You are beating a dead horse if you keep doing what you are doing with whom you are doing it and maintain having to deal with consequence instead of reward. Some people thrive on this type environment but look at them. It is not a myth that there is good and evil in the world. "Good" and "Evil" can merely be replaced with the words "Positive" and "Negative" or "Affirmed" and "Unaffirmed." It is a matter of perception.

Perception is such an important part of living and can encompass the results of value judging, fear, criticism and praise, to name a few. Perception is not a positive or a negative. It is what it is-a perception. People mistake them for opinions or fact and conflict arises because two or more viewpoints collide. Perception is not meant to be a positive or negative. It is true and valid for each person. The definition of perception is the understanding or knowledge of an idea, concept or impression so formed. If you break this definition down, maybe you can see how perceptions could create the problems even when they were not meant to create difficulty.

Let us take "understanding of an idea or impression" to start. This is to know the meaning of our impression. This is from our learned background. Perception is learned and created from our unique and different awareness pools. Our awareness pool is only as expansive as our awareness. Our awareness is created from our heredity, intuitions, and total life experiences to date. Tomorrow will be different than today. If we have few total life experiences to add to our pool and our heredity has also limited our growth, then it would be safe to say that our perceptions could be limited as well.

Many perceptions are passed down through the generations. The cycle of recipients have not experienced anything differently, so they make that "handed down" perception part of their history and keep passing it on. Perceptions are not fact. Let me make that clear. There are no right or wrong perceptions. Perceptions are impressions based on criteria experienced and the conclusion for one person does not make it a conclusion for another. Times and situations change, so using a *handed down* perception doesn't even make sense. Take a look at the history of theologians and religions that have interpreted the meaning of the Bible. Why do you think there are so many factions of religion? Because the perceptions of interpretation are different, therefore, creating a new religious faction to fit the perception. And like other perceptions, they usually conflict with another's belief system. This can cause wars and has caused wars.

If you scale this down to relationships, one person calculates the facts from their knowledge base and goes up against another who calculates it from their own knowledge base. Wham! Everybody is unique, so the perceptions will be unique. The conflicts arise because people don't want to listen to the other's unique reasons for what they perceive. You are basically saying you don't care about their knowledge base of experiences. You must have the only correct path in the world! No one wants to take the time to understand another's perception. You also don't have to agree, just understand.

There are times when there is a no-win result because people will not compromise or accept that they don't agree. They get angry and become bitter. You either withdraw and accept their position as theirs and know they have to deal with the reality of their beliefs or find ways to continue compromising. If it does not have a direct effect on your life, then my suggestion would be to withdraw because it is not your reality.

Ego is the only reason people keep hammering away and we have learned that ego is a mask for low self-esteem.

How many times have you perceived something about someone only to find out through more information that person isn't what you thought? It can go either way, positive or negative. I have met people that were dressed with the finest of clothing and a charisma that would knock you dead. As time went by, I realized they were the biggest scams in town. All that glitters is not gold. My perception changed after new information. I have also seen the opposite. An old gentleman came into a dealership in overalls, flannel shirt and boots. The salespeople ignored him and went toward the people that looked like they could buy a car. The owner happened to see the gentleman and struck up a conversation with him in a very friendly manner. To make a long story short, the gentleman bought two Zimmers at $65,000 a piece and paid cash. Well, whose perception was distorted?

The point of these stories is to make you stop and think before you judge, criticize or blame someone who does not fit your criteria. Perfection is in the eye of the beholder and faulty perceptions are easily developed to distort what is truth. Truth can be unique for everyone as perception is unique to everyone. Perfection is an illusion. If something is perfect, change is not necessary. I love the saying "Green apples grow and ripe apples rot." Life is ever changing and growing toward perfection. How can we expect our perceptions to be the perfect solution for everyone? Everyone grows at a different rate. Love is the only perfect thing in life and we are a far cry from reaching that goal universally. When perceptions can be allowed and aligned to win-win solutions, we will be on our way to reaching the goal of loving.

Whenever you feel you have no choices, this is a faulty perception. This is either a trick you play on yourself or it is someone else's attempts to make you feel inadequate. It could be avoidance of responsibility for taking action. Others will try to pound their perceptions at you to keep you off balance and therefore creating conflict for yourself. It is your choice, your choice, your choice! Envision what you want, play with the different ways of achieving it, have conviction and follow your own intuition for direction. How others perceive your actions is their responsibility, not yours to prove to them. If they are truly interested in your happiness, they will not stand in your way.

This is why it is so important to increase your self awareness. Nothing can occur in your life that isn't your choice. If you accept other's words blindly as truth, you will fall into the pity pot of self-destructive judgment of yourself and others. Your attitude cannot possibly change because you are living in another's reality. So what is it to be? Sitting and waiting for praise and approval or take hold of your life and know you don't need someone's praise and approval? Be happy with yourself.

If I get nothing else across in this book, I hope you can learn to be honest with what you truly desire and take responsibility for your choices. Do not allow the chains of faulty awareness and control of your emotional guilts to keep you from your goals. Your attitude will change toward the positive because you will become independent. The shackles will drop off and you will feel so much lighter. What you perceive will be and what you believe shall be perceived.

Chapter 12
Stress and Your Health

I was taught by one of my mentors that stress is responsible for 97% of all illness. I was young when I learned this fact and it took many years to observe this fact as truth. It is my nature to accept information into my brain to observe first and then make my own conclusions. Sometimes ten years pass before I see the truth in a statement, but eventually it proves itself one way or the other.

If illness is caused by stress, then let us go back to what causes stress. Stress is caused by what we are thinking about at the time that may conflict with another person or situation. Things are not in alignment for a smooth flow of positive energy. It is like running an automobile. If one part of the car wears out or quits, the rest of the car becomes inoperable and needs fixed with a timely approach. If you wait too long to get it fixed, it could cause more damage and cost more time and money to repair.

Your mind and body run the same way. One does not work without the other. The importance of maintaining a healthy mind and body is essential. The mind is the priority because it rules the body. It sends the signals based on what your thoughts express. What your thoughts express is what your body perceives as truth. Your body is a result of what you think consciously or unconsciously. It is these thoughts of fear and doubt that sabotage the thoughts of success and health. So, when your mind becomes "needy," your body becomes "needy." If your mind tells you that you have too much weight on the body, your body perceives that very idea and helps create that very scenario. If you want to reverse the process, start believing that you will be thin through desire, discipline, flexibility and faith.

Again, the commitment and action are necessary once you get out of the mourning stages of denial and bargaining. You need to re-program your mind to create a new you. The problem is allowing people to divert you and control you by offering you that big piece of chocolate cake causing the conflict inside you because you are still "shaky" on the path of feeling good.

How many times have you been thrown off course because of a breakup in a relationship, work is unbearable or something stresses you out? We slip back because we are not honest with ourselves and don't really want to commit. The desire is not great enough to succeed. Your body is the only one that knows you are lying and so it still creates the original results. We get caught up in the problems keeping us from our goals and the problems become more important than our goals. Your body is smarter than you think or even knew.

I did not have health insurance for at least 20 years. I really wasn't concerned for some reason because I had told myself that I couldn't afford to get sick and I never did get sick. I had sinus problems, but I could live with that. I didn't really want to pay the high prices anyway. I occasionally allow others to put that doubt of "not having" into my head. "You never know when you might need it." I guess I will have to write another book when I am old to let you know how I did.

Disease and sickness are created by thoughts of fear. You fear getting cancer, you get cancer. The media doesn't help much with this matter. They are constantly letting us know the percentages of people getting a disease. Stress allows the door to open for disease. The media plants that fear with every commercial announcement, medical study and obituary. My mentor suggested we not read the paper or watch TV because it thrives on the negative. The old shows were geared more toward happiness and healthiness in relationships and jobs and left out all of the "blood and guts" as it were. It is all right to acknowledge services available, but do we have to create a commercial with someone sitting there with a forlorn face suffering from overeating?

I was involved, at one time, in a news fiasco, which made national news. The media created a high profile situation without disclosing all of the facts of the situation and their twisted illusion of the situation caused me to get death threats every five minutes at my job. The media was not interested in the truth, only what sells. As you can see, I do not have much respect for the direction media takes us when they could be used as a powerful tool toward the positive.

What about studies that eggs were bad for us? One year later, they were good for us again. So what is a person to do? Listen to your own body. Eat in moderate and balanced portions. Excess of anything is not good. If your life is balanced, you will not be "needy" for excess of anything.

I also experienced the death of a woman who had excessively deep wrinkles in her face. When she passed over the most amazing thing happened! Her wrinkles disappeared! I remember thinking "My God, this is amazing!" I thought the wrinkles were just from age, but when they disappeared, I knew it was from stress. Her stress now gone so went the wrinkles and the skin looked almost youthful again.

Changing what you eat may make you feel differently, but if you do not change your outlook and attitude to one of a positive nature, your body is going to be the road map of all that is hidden, like it or not. All those repressed angers, frustrations, conflicts and poisoned thoughts keep showing up physically on us. Start taking inventory of your unproductive thoughts that keeps propagating repeatedly. Repetitive thoughts will eventually and severely affect the nervous system and create chemical dependencies, mood disorders and depressions. I don't know how many times I met someone to find out their age was 20 years older. Whew! Talk about being put away wet!

Start to take inventory of your thoughts and listen to what comes out of your mouth. Is it opinionated, negative, value judging or criticizing? Do you say, "I am no good, I can't lose weight, nothing works, why try-nobody cares?" or "that person is self absorbed, a know it all, an idiot."

Evaluate how many positives come out of your mouth versus how many negatives and I think you could get ill just hearing yourself speak. You can worry in a good way, but envy, jealousy and disappointment you exude will rob your body of positive and healthy nutrients of youth and grace.

Just because someone has a history of family depression and disease only means the same thoughts are passed down each generation. There are genetic disorders, which may need care, but if it is an emotional situation due to behavioral conditioning, you can control the outcomes. It is easy, but not simple. If you are expecting it to happen to you because it happened to them, you will probably be even worse because the more you anticipate the fear of it; the more likely the disease is to surface sooner.

There will be obstacles to overcome. Some of the obstacles will be worse for some than others. Some of the obstacles are illusions set before you and how you perceive this is up to you. You can let the images and thoughts control you and your health or you can control your health by replacing the old thoughts with new ones. You are the mother, father and child to yourself. What kind of family are you going to create?

For those of you with serious emotional, physical or chemical abuse in your background, there is hope for you. Please seek counsel with someone that *feels* right with your energy. Not every combination of Doctor/patient is the most effective for your particular situation. Ask questions and you will know if that person is the right one for you. There are also groups that are formed that specialize in certain areas. Again, find the group that fits you. I have heard people say they went to a group and it was horrible and never went back again. Maybe that wasn't the right energy source. I went with a friend to an AA meeting once and it was the most boring and depressed meeting I had ever seen. It was a large group, too. I couldn't wait to get out of there. The negative underlying energy at this particular meeting was strong. It seemed to me these people were dwelling on the problem with no solutions or education on re-programming to the positive. They were all sucking down coffee and smoking cigarettes trying to get rid of the urges.

My point is find a group that would align with what feels right for you if a group is what helps you. Sometimes our peers are our best teachers and with a positive support system, overcoming a difficulty can be much easier. You certainly don't need someone who pushes your buttons and causes you to regress. Don't attempt to avoid or hide from the issues that need changing because your body will not lie. It will know when you are faking.

Chapter 13
Anxiety

Let us talk about anxiety for a minute. Anxiety is one of the most important concepts in the psychoanalytic philosophy. It plays an important role in the development of personality functioning. Anxiety is a painful emotional experience, which is triggered by internal or external stimuli and runs through the nervous system.

Anxiety is different from the other painful states of tension, pain and depression because it is a conscious state of mind. Anxiety is a result of feeling the other types of pain, which could be affected by hunger, thirst and other bodily needs. There is no such thing as an unconscious anxiety. You have to experience anxiety for it to exist. You can experience clammy hands, dry throat and racing heartbeats as examples.

Anxiety is parallel to fear. Fear has been discussed in earlier chapters and the effects fear has on our attitudes, health and mental stability. Anxiety is painful, but is necessary as a danger signal to the conscious mind so the mind can create measures to deal with the danger. You can then ward off danger by identifying whether it is externally or internally stimulated. It if is not taken care of, anxiety can layer itself to the point of a person becoming overwhelmed. Then you might have a nervous breakdown. Remember, I said that anxiety runs through the nervous system. You short circuit. You may experience danger by physically harming yourself or you may experience physical harm directly from someone which would be considered external stimuli. If you perceive danger, your anxiety is triggered. Whether it is learned or acquired from heredity or both, you feel helplessness as a child would feel because you have not learned to cope with all of the stimuli yet. This is why children need to be shielded from too many negative stimuli in the beginning because their coping skills are not adequate to handle all of the stimuli.

All fears begin in childhood and as you get older, any situation that would reduce you back to the state of helplessness as a child will trigger the anxiety flag. If you have not learned appropriate coping skills along the way, it can build up to a major collapse. It can kill you if there is no release valve to regulate self-protective behavior. This is why in adulthood, you either handle stress and anxiety well or you don't. If you grew up in a very dysfunctional family where physical, sexual and /or verbal abuse was present on a daily basis, you didn't have time or the chance to learn to cope or to heal in time for the next trauma. This becomes "Normal behavior" and you learn to abuse yourself or others as you get older. You do not know what coping even has to do with the situation.

It is not a hopeless situation if caught early on. It can be unlearned and re-taught. The older you get, the more difficult it becomes because it has become imprinted into your psyche and has started to effect you physically as well. The problems become more numerous. I personally believe a person can continue to try to achieve little successes if it hasn't become a permanently damaged situation. The goal is to take as many steps forward as possible. Illness is the confusion of that particular person manifesting the new mental imprint physically so the conscious can see it. Your body vibrates to the stress. Pay attention and ask yourself what your spirit needs.

You can also experience fears and anxieties in the form of phobias, which are irrational fears. This is when the fear is out of proportion to the danger. You can have panic attacks, which come up out of nowhere. This can cause a person who has built up an excessive amount of anxiety to gun down people they do not know just to rid themselves of their own painful anxiety. They found a negative release valve. This is an extreme case, but it can also surface simply as an impulsive statement that is out of character. Everyone can experience an anxiety. The differences in people's reactions are based on the way they were taught to cope and for some that was none at all.

The neurotic person has learned no control. They react impulsively and that usually winds up getting them in trouble. The point is to restate that fear and understand anxiety can be good if you can heed the warning signal of apprehension and caution. You then utilize your coping skills to divert the intensity levels to controllable reactions. The level of intensity and fear and the perception of the fear being real or imagined will be apparent in your behavior and attitudes.

I still believe the majority of neuroses and psychoses originated at a young age by negative traumatic stimuli, which continued to layer over the years, and the recipients just short-circuited. Their nervous system could not handle it. There are so many medications available now that can actually help smooth these circuits out to balance the brain functions so people can think more clearly and learn to cope at a lower intensity level. It is not the cure all though. Education needs to assist in the transformation.

You can help the process if you can eat, think and be healthy. Listen to your body and your instincts. Your body will warn you if you listen. If you say, "why bother" you are allowing outside forces to control you. Failure, negativity, trauma, danger and frustrations create blockages in the personality. Resistance and irritations are results, which cause anxiety and tension. It also reduces our level of awareness in making wise decisions for ourselves. Positive successes, victories and achievements will favor the mind to function more freely and allow our instinctual psychic abilities to guide us in a positive direction with less tension and anxiety.

Chapter 14
Your Own Therapist

We have talked about how fear and anxiety can actually be helpful in identifying the direction we take or decisions we make. They are part of our "inner knower" or intuition. This is a part of ourselves we tend to ignore because we have been conditioned to ignore it. We have been taught to doubt our intuition by allowing others to make our decisions for us. The fear and anxiety are actually the "red flags" we need that warn us that we are not following our own "inner knower."

There are actually three aspects to our personal awareness. The first is our heredity, which cannot be changed. The second is our total life experiences, which are unique to each person and also include all external stimuli from every environment, situation and person we have encountered. This is constantly changing every second of the day. The third is our inner knower or intuitions, as you are more familiar, which is ours and ours alone. This is the hidden gift God has given each of us that is there for life. It can be justified, ignored, tested, doubted, cursed and silent, but at any time it can come through for you. It cannot be erased or stolen, but it can be resisted.

Everyone at some point in their life has experienced the feeling of "I was going to say that" or "I had thought of that, but I didn't act." How many times have you kicked yourself for not following your hunch? That is your intuition working. I have done it more times than I care to count and still miss the information from time to time. In fact, I have asked for help in writing this particular chapter because I know this is an intangible, yet so important an aspect which needs to be addressed. The help I am asking is from my own inner knower, not another person. So, bare with me and we will see how this chapter flows.

I am going to try and explain as simply as possible so that you can relate from your own experiences and remember the instances which you knew were your own voices. It is very important to know these voices never, never speak in a negative, hurtful or painful manner toward you and never ask or tell you to do anything that causes pain to yourself or others. Remember, this is your direct line to God and God does not ever ask of you to follow through with revengeful acts or any acts that involve negative results. If you are hearing negative voices, then I would suggest seeing a psychiatrist to help you identify the origin of these messages. I believe that you are hearing some "old tapes" playing from distorted childhood experiences that need to be changed or there is an underlying reason that a specialist can help you sort out. Either way, you need to remain in the positive frame of reference, which is simple, but not easy. A lot of people have had to endure negative reinforcing which has caused the "beautiful voices" to lay dormant and unheard. The wondrous thing is they are still there waiting to be heard!

That is the beauty of the inner knower. It is your personal therapist if you allow it to work for you. It takes practice, testing and patience to receive the messages. Your spiritual teachers are ready and will be joyful when you puncture through the darkness and allow the light to shine through.

The only tools you need are yourself and a quiet, safe and uninterrupted space. You sit back and become calm.

Accept nothing that does not sound right to you. That is your responsibility and must not ever be given to another person for their approval or input. You are defeating the whole process when you give power away to another. Until you are strong enough to accept the messages without question, it would actually be beneficial for you to not disclose to others your insights because you open yourself up to doubt.

Now, without opening myself up to be diagnosed, I will tell you that I have reached the point of having aggressive conversations with my inner knower, out loud sometimes, so I can hear and focus better on the responses. I do not do this in the presence of others or I am sure they would lock me up for having an imaginary friend. Which, by the way, just might be the friend your children talk to when they are so young. They are a clear channel for the inner knower because they haven't the clutter to get in the way. Anyway, it is a private matter and when my external environment is too distracting or noisy, I take a deep breath and say "O.K. What are you trying to tell me?" I listen to the first thing I hear. If I find myself arguing with the message, I eventually catch myself and realize I am justifying my position. Sometimes, the answer isn't what I want, because I am sometimes determined to take the wrong path and am too stubborn to admit when the voices are correct. So, I ignore the message; do what I want because it is my right to choose, and later, when I fall on my face say "I knew I should have done what they told me or *what I originally thought.*"

Your inner knower is not going to yell at you through your resistance. It will sit back and wait for you to eat your own decision. It will allow you to make mistakes if that is what it takes for you to start trusting yourself. If you keep doing what you are doing, you will keep getting what you are getting. Heard this before? Your inner knower has unconditional patience even if it takes a lifetime or several for you to finally hear. For some people it may take an eternity or until they just get tired of being sick and tired.

Do you remember the saying "Out of the mouths of babes?" Children are the true channels for truth and always say the first thing that comes to mind. It is the parent that starts to alter the natural channels of truth and inhibits the nurturing of the gift we were all given. If you take the time to ask a child why they said something, their usual reply is "I don't know why," or they say, "my imaginary friend told me to say it." Maybe their imaginary friend is their inner knower and they are so in tuned they can see as well as hear their guide from the spirit world. The child hasn't the stress or the clutter to resist anything until the adults begin to fill up those spaces with their clutter.

So what do we do when the child says something out of "the air" that speaks of truth? We laugh, get embarrassed or angry depending on what comes out of the child's mouth. I will give an example from my life experience when I was very young, I believe around five or six. An Aunt came to take care of my brothers and I for a week in the summer. I don't remember where my parents went. She was a very contrary and grumpy woman. She yelled at us for opening the door numerous times in the day to go in and out of the house. Each time was a different reason. "You are letting the cold air out or the hot air in." My brothers and I were crazy, but we maintained our dignity and respect until my parents came home.

Upon their return, my father asked Aunt Fanny when she would like to be taken home and on the tail end of her response, I said, "it is about time!!!" Well, I was only speaking the truth of an unbearable situation for all. My father hustled me down to the basement landing where I was told never to speak again in the presence of adults and I was to apologize.

From that point, my inner knower became a mute. My ability to speak freely had been altered so harshly, that I used to cry when I was confronted to speak the truth to someone when it needed to be spoken. If my parents had guided me through the process of controlling the words of truth instead of making the truth hurt, I may not have spent most of my twenties taking public speaking courses to be able to speak freely and confidently again. I could have learned appropriate responses and not "freeze up" every time things needed to be said. I second-guessed myself so much I couldn't even find words. Therefore, I became shy. This is certainly not to say I didn't need to learn to be a little more quiet and not so blunt and assured. I still have that problem today and I have to discern when it is right to speak and when not to speak. Some things we carry with us.

The point of the story is it takes many years for your inner knower to reach its own identity and it takes time to understand and refine the raw "blurbs" that immerse from a child. When peers cause confusion for you without understanding of the lesson, you begin to doubt your truth instead of learning to use the truth at an appropriate time and manner. You should not be denounced when you are learning the steps to refinement. You then become fearful of taking risks for you can't hear the voices anymore for the clutter of doubt and confusion in your head.

I discussed a process in an earlier chapter about making decisions using your inner knower as your guide. It envelops your intellect and your feelings. Your inner knower comes in many forms. Some people hear messages and some feel messages. I use both to my advantage as you can as well. It can come through dreams, a line in a movie, and a chorus of a song. If it touches a chord in you that makes sense and gives you a confident direction, it is your inner knower. If it clears out the confusion, fear and doubt, it is your inner knower. Fear is only an empty room of illusion. It is not reality. Your inner knower is a reality. It exists and it can be measured with results.

As I have said earlier, making the correct decision for you will bring feelings of freedom, lightness and movement forward. It will create an excitement of knowingness. It will be motivating. A decision, which is incorrect for you will make you feel tense, awkward, unsure, fearful, and resistant to that direction. You will feel fight and/or flight. Take an example from your life that you have already experienced. Let us say a relationship that you know is over. Form a question from this experience. "Should I get back into a relationship with this individual or not??" Separate this question into two questions. "Should I get back into this relationship with..." and "Should I stay out of this relationship with...and move on?" Now, you know the correct answer intellectually. Use your feelings to answer the rest of the query. We have discussed this process already.

Which answer gives you a free flowing and light feeling of knowingness? Which one makes you feel free, warm and secure? Which answer makes you feel tense at the thought of going in that direction? Which answer makes you cringe and wrinkle your face? Do you see what I mean by paying attention to your body? You have used an experience that you know the outcome. You get an honest and truthful direction from your body because you have experienced it already.

This system works when you do not know the outcome. You have to pay close attention to your feelings. This can be difficult at first, but practice will enable you to do this instantaneously and with confidence. The best way to learn is by using experiences you know the outcome to remember the feelings and then formulate your questions to the new situation having more confidence in your responses. Remember to make each question one direction. "Would it be best for me to move to Colorado?" "Would it be best for me to stay in San Diego?" "Would it be best for me to wait until next year to make a decision?" Each question should be clearly defined with one direction. You can have as many directions as you want, but always in a separate question. Feel the answers. Play with the process daily. Every decision you make, feel your way to the answer. Try not to intellectualize because you run the risk of letting the clutter make your decisions. Your inner knower is your best teacher and your best therapist. It doesn't cost you anything and you can do it quietly anywhere you like and at any time.

Chapter 15
Three Biggest Fears

We need each other to survive. We have certain needs and desires that cause us to interact with each other and the way we interact has a profound effect on our mental health. Our mental health in turn, has an effect on our physical well-being. There have been studies that prove people who have a positive closeness and kindness for each other live longer and are better able to cope with stress. Anxiety and depression are created from isolation and loneliness because people do not know how to interact in a healthy manner.

It is difficult to interact in a healthy manner if we are not mentally healthy ourselves. I have discussed the aspects of fear, anger and value judging of ourselves and others and the responses stirred up when we engage in conflict. Understanding conflict is necessary and understanding positive relationships is easy to verbalize, but less simple to put into play.

As in any relationship, everyone needs to feel good. In the art of negotiations, we need to create win-win outcomes. The factors for creating win-win situations of any kind begin with *listening*. Other factors include honesty and being able to express honest feelings to another person. If we do not know what we want, then we allow others to make our decisions for us. We usually end up with a win-lose situation. I know no one has ever been in that situation before, right?

There are three counterproductive behaviors that create poor interpersonal communications. They are the three biggest fears we have that can actually traumatize some people to the point of sabotaging closeness and giving up on themselves completely. They are, fear of abandonment, rejection and fear of failure. People fail to take charge of their lives to change and minimize their risk-taking because of these three aspects. Some people will give up who they are because they are afraid someone will leave them, or not give them the approval they need to be themselves.

Others will initiate steps to create the outcomes of not being loved, push the ones closest to them away or fail at everything because that is what they expect will eventually happen anyway. The results are the same for both, very depressed people who are frustrated and angry. Remember that anger is a cover for fear and each fear trails back to one of the big three.

There is an appropriate time and place to communicate. You don't take your personal issues to work and monopolize everyone's time and energy. You don't monopolize your friends' time when they may have their own issues. You need to listen once in awhile to see what boundaries are present. There may be people who you trust that do have the time and energy, but you must observe the boundaries so it doesn't turn into a control issue or a battle of values and neediness. Know what you need before you disclose and know how much you can accept from the other person. If this is not established up front, guilt, remorse and shame can surface and then anger. You start blaming yourself or them if information gets out of control or twisted. Do not feel you need to tell everything because you are seeking that approval or commiseration of someone else to justify how you feel. That is not healthy either. Remember that fear is an illusion; so the big three are illusions as well. It is all in how you perceive a situation.

If you are fearful of abandonment or rejection from people closest to you, then check your behavior and see what you are doing to create the situation to happen. Are you being mistrustful, jealous, and non-attentive or judging their every action? Are these things going to keep someone happy or push them away? If you cannot love without strings attached, please take a look at the strings that bind because those will be the fears reaching out from your being as a need. Is that need becoming neediness?

People do not know what to make of conflict. We all know it is uncomfortable and painful. Many have been conditioned to avoid conflict when growing up. Some were taught to hit it head on. I believe a happy median is the most beneficial, because I believe in balance. Our conditioning has convinced us to deny our feelings for the sake of peace. How is that win-win? Everyone is that unique snowflake with different thoughts, desires and needs, so how could there never be conflict? People can still disagree and create a win-win outcome. It is the attitude you choose to adopt when you are listening to the other person's side. Dealing with conflict is a skill that can be learned. If you maintain the attitude that no one else could possibly have a valid thought of their own, then you will always end your relationships in a destructive manner.

It is important the other party understands clearly and there is no double message. This requires you to be clear with yourself first. Everything keeps circling back around to you again. Know yourself clearly and you will express more clearly and confidently. Don't allow others to speak for you and allow others to speak for themselves. It takes some people a long time to get it out, so be patient. Have respect and listen when they do finally speak. Clarify as the conversation continues in a non-threatening manner, as you would want someone to handle you. Do not monopolize, side step their issues or judge what they are saying as wrong. You can expect rejection for sure if you start that game. Take responsibility for your feelings, not theirs. They own their feelings; you don't own them. You can respect their feelings with sincerity when you let go of your fears of a defensive perspective.

Conflict arises when people need to resolve different views. You can run from them or deal with it constructively without fear of conflict. You only fear that which is unknown, so open up and be honest so the unknown is less of a threat. If you are uncertain of the trust issue or the sincerity of a person truly wanting to create a win-win situation, you may need to discern whether it is worth wasting your time. I have been in situations before where I tried every way I could think and the person did not budge from their position or make any concessions.

It was definitely "beating a dead horse" situation. That is when you pack up or smile and say, "See ya." I think enough of myself to find another environment that is conducive to my growth and happiness. I do not fear the abandonment, but welcome it. I am not fearful of rejection because I did all I could do and more to make it right. It just wasn't meant to be. Maybe the other person was creating the scenario to feed their own fears of rejection and abandonment and it worked for them.

Chapter 16
Trust is Scary

I find that people who are depressed are fearful of trusting people as well as themselves. They have chosen to hide the negative parts of them for fear of being found out. They are either ashamed or embarrassed to let others see them for who they really are underneath the masks they carry. They will lie and make up stories to cover their faulty behaviors. They will start creating their own reality, which can become delusional if carried too far.

Children are wide open with honesty. They have no problem "laying the cards out on the table" even if they hurt someone's feelings in the process. They do not understand boundaries, yet. They have no problem expressing anger, fear, love or any other emotions directly. This is refreshing at times but does need to be refined along the way.

Hopefully, with the proper training, children are guided to understand appropriate timing and words to express feelings in a productive way. Usually, they are made to feel guilty or ashamed and begin to suppress. We know what happens when we reach adolescent or adult age. We create an escape of our choosing to numb what we don't want to feel or fill a void of not knowing what we are feeling. Some become alcoholics, shoplifters, drug users, depressed or whatever it takes to have a crutch. The crutch is used to not have to face ourselves and the possible "flaws" that have accumulated over the years.

The masks serve us well until they become a problem with major consequences of physical or mental breakdown.

There are certain areas of human interactive and social relations, which can be described about awareness of ourselves. We have hidden realities that we may not see about ourselves, but others may see. We are always expressing ourselves through body language and our masks aren't always full proof. People can actually see through another's mask at times. Otherwise, the only way we find out about these areas is if one or more people bring it to our attention or we have the guts to ask how others perceive us. Sometimes, we just choose not to see how we are being perceived.

The larger the mask we carry, the more lies we tell and the more energy we use up in a non-productive way. We need to create opportunities to open the lines of communication so we can change in positive ways. If we choose to remain in the dark and are not able to acknowledge that we are having ill thoughts, it will manifest again and again. Having insight to your negative feelings allows you to handle things in a more productive say. Awareness of your problems allows you to become more open to growth and change.

There are, of course, unknown factors, which always exist, and much of the time it is because people do not communicate anything of their feelings with each other, so they are both in the dark. The point is, the unknown is still affecting relations in some way. Carrying masks or not communicating anything is a lot of non-productive energy and becomes a weight of fear, anxiety, and insecurity, which puts people into a hole not to trust. If you learn more about yourself by reducing the "hidden zones" and taking a risk to change behavior, your unknown areas will diminish and your fear of people and yourself will also diminish. You will begin to trust more and your depressive isolation from others will give way to more freedom.

Suppose you have gone to a party where you know very few people. Your trust level is minimal when you first get there. You have to observe body languages and verbal interactions before you size up if you are going to stay or not. If you have a few pleasant experiences in the beginning, you begin to trust more and move around more freely to a level of your comfort. You have more pleasant experiences, which find you actually laughing and initiating conversation.

What happens if you meet someone who makes you uncomfortable? Do you judge the whole party on the one incident? That would depend on your self-esteem. To some, this might devastate them to the point of leaving the party quietly and not attending another party for a long time. That person becomes paranoid that everyone saw how inadequate they were and sure everyone noticed and was talking about them. To be able to recognize an isolated incident that could have been dealt with using clearly defined communication techniques is a self esteem issue which turns into a trust issue. Do you trust yourself enough to know the difference or do you run because you don't have confidence in your abilities? The layering of these incidences could cause a person to close off and become lonely and depressed.

Loneliness is merely a lack of trust. A person is fearful of being hurt or rejected or made to feel guilty about the way they have developed. You fear to be wrong. You fear to love in an imperfect world. Think of that. Is everyone around you perfect? I think not! If they are giving that impression, I suggest you relax and know that person is pulling the wool over your eyes. Everyone has issues to overcome. Everyone. The world is perfectly imperfect. Without deficiency, there would be no growth possibility.

The flowers, water, animals, and humans are created perfect, but they are always changing in some way. They are refined to create new perfection. The cycles of the seasons are orderly and consistent, but they change. We can trust that the weather will change and all living things will adjust accordingly. We are the only creatures that have been given "choices" and can make the changes consciously. So it is choice to create trust. We were close to that many years ago when the United States was new. People had to develop trust and ban together to survive. Once people put down roots, they become protective and fearful of losing again. Yet, they took the risk to lose it all to get to that point.

Material things can all be taken away with or without the help of the untrustworthy. If attachment to anyone or anything limits you and you become "safe" where you choose to stop growing, you start to lose yourself. If you do not continue to reach out to another and trust in the higher power to guide you through the trials and the risks, there will be no human community. The nations will find each other someday when they realize the need for all is far greater and more powerful than the need for one to be alone.

If you sit depressed and lonely, look at your trust level and see what value you have placed on these issues or what someone else has placed there for you. You can change all of that! Venture out more, look up when you walk, turn your head and see what is around you. Find the humor and the beauty. You are where you are supposed to be and experiencing that which you are to experience. It enhances your awareness and in turn, your growth of self. No matter how far your life seems to drift, make the trip. There is a reason for it. Enjoy and trust and learn.

Chapter 17
Who Are You?

When do we lose ourselves? When do we know who we really are or have we ever been our real self? How many of you can say "I know who I am and where I want to go?" I doubt there are many who are sure, but that is truly our purpose in life. We mistake our purpose for accumulation of material things and yet how many have said "is this all there is once they get it?" The hole is still there. It is inside of us as intangible as ever.

Some say they can't feel anything and never have been able to feel anything. Some say they have no goals and some say they have no passions. They feel all has been lost. Nothing is really lost, only hidden. How many hold onto relationships or situations that they are unhappy maintaining? What are they giving value to that could limit their growth or the growth of the people involved? Maybe fear is truly the reason. This life is for learning, growing and taking risks. If you want to change and the other people are not changing and growing with you and you have done all you can do, then maybe it is time to move on. No matter what the cost! You lose temporarily, but will gain in the end. If there are children involved, did you ever stop to think what example you are showing them? You may be showing them it is okay to settle for less of yourself to be happy with the money and things that have been accumulated together. Your self does not matter anymore. It is for the "family." You might have a chance to find what true happiness is if you give yourself permission to feel happiness.

You may become fixated on things, become more needy for things and cling onto that which you think is providing those things. You start to suffocate the person and end up draining the life out of the relationship. Creativity is stressed and you and the other person start to withdraw. You are breeding inappropriate instruction to your children on what is meant to be. I am not suggesting breaking up a family without making attempts to create a healthy environment for all, but if all parties are not participating equally and attaching strings are so tight one cannot breathe, maybe the best decision is to move on.

Reality is "this situation is making me sad, angry or just plain unhappy and maybe I need to make some changes.' The old way is to force something to work to save face. How can this be living? I was told once that if you have to fight to get something you have to fight to keep it as well. I have found this to be true. If it is a job, relationship or money, the natural flow of obtaining that, which feels right and correct, is a much more stress free approach than forcing the square peg in the round hole. I am sure the challenge would give some a feeling of achievement until you realize there is a lot of unused space surrounding it. When you try to pull the round peg out, it is damaged and sometimes irreparable. There could be extra crud that has filtered into the loose spaces causing it to rot if left too long. How long are you going to be the square peg in the round hole? Have you figured out that you don't fit? Have you become comfortable being uncomfortable? We become comfortable because we are stuck or we feel it is too much effort to look for the proper fit.

Sometimes, we give up because the force is too much. If others have beaten you into the hole where your whole being is distorted, you may not recognize the opportunities that have passed you by because you have become so insecure and feeling that this is what is to be. You become crystallized and blinded to the beauty that may be around the corner. It requires risk and letting go of the old to let the new in. You need to find the force that is flowing with you, not against you. Remember, we do make mistakes. We are human. We usually do not *find ourselves* until later in life, so everything to that point is to help guide you there. Every experience is to help you see what you don't want as well as what you do want. Are you willing to trust faith and be guided toward the appropriate job or relationship or do you choose to stay stuck and unchangeable?

If you choose to stay stuck, then you will continue to remain miserable and wondering "what if?" I will say this over and over. Learn about yourself and what makes you happy and happiness will follow. The higher your self-esteem, the less people can control you and how you feel. When you reach the goal of self, you will be able to see it in another person as well and the chemistry will blend smoothly and freely. If you have doubt about who you are and what you want, people will manipulate you, control you and make you feel worthless. They will say "Can't you think for yourself, Go find something to do that makes you happy, Quit expecting me to have all the answers, Do this, do that." You are always going to hear some comment, which is directed toward yourself. Then you become hurt and anger sets in. You had best be grounded or you will spend your life jumping from person to person, situation to situation, job to job and you will stay stuck in misery wondering what the "thing" is that is good for you. You begin to complain, nag, value judge and the process of deterioration begins.

Start spending some time with yourself. Set aside time for yourself. Try new things or go to new places that are different than what you are used to seeing. Experience new things. How will you ever know if you don't do it? Some things you will like and some you won't. That is part of the journey! How simple! Part of it is finding out what you like and what you dislike. It is not to find out what someone else likes or dislikes or whether they will or won't follow you. It is best to find this out before you cohabit because the "red flags" will fly high. You can eliminate a lot of heartache if you take time in the beginning.

When you are young, you feel sure you know what it is you want and no one can stop you. That is okay because life will test that and it can be blunt about it. If you spend your journey on someone else's path, your Self is only going through the motions or emotions and your joy of life is lost. When you find your joy, the right person will see the glow in you and want to follow alongside at the same speed. What makes you happy will free up your creativity and your desires will glow brightly.

Trust in yourself even if it feels like you have to reinvent yourself. Someone has already tried to mold us in their eyes and see how we feel? Now it is time to mold ourselves. Step outside and start exploring like the child you still have inside. Buy a coloring book and color! Read a children's book that you always wanted to read and never did! Sit in the sand or snow and make "angels." They really do exist if you believe and know how to recognize them.

Chapter 18
Heal Thyself

Do you want to be healed? Do you have the belief that you can heal yourself? It is a concept that seems too farfetched to believe we can control our destinies of wellness. We can. There are people who wish not to be healed. They have created their own block to learning through illness. Illness is the body's expression of confusion of the soul. The illness is actually a release valve for people to counteract the blockage to avoid learning anymore about certain factors of their life. Emotional problems with no coping ability attached can get severe enough to cause a person to go insane from fear. Insanity means the negative won. It is a form of ultimate trauma without a means to cope. People have to learn to deal with fear early on because it is a form of denial and denial strangles the physical body. If your soul chooses to live, healing begins. Denial diminishes. Your conscious mind makes a decision and commitment to beat the disease. I have been taught that to force healing on someone who is not ready to heal is to inflict my will on them. One has to want to change.

You could beat a dead horse to get it to move before you realize your energy could be used on a more productive situation. I would like to think we can make a difference and we can, but the guilt and stress that go along with trying to change someone who does not really care whether they change is stressful. You cannot motivate anyone: *only provide the environment which they can discover their own motivation*. The same is with illness. You cannot heal someone; *only provide them with the love and support to help them heal themselves.* I am sure that many may question this philosophy, but I know people have tried to motivate me in the past and I don't budge unless I feel the interest within myself first.

Our bodies create the physical manifestation of the illness of fear, which we do not want to face. If we can face the truth of the cause, we can understand it, learn from it and let it go. Pain is a red flag. It tells us what we are resisting or denying. Stress causes the concentration to form in the weakest part of bodies. The more we deny, the greater the stress on that area.

Most people have a very difficult time facing things and letting go. We hold onto things, people and memories out of duty, obligation or fear that we will lose something. It is said that new things cannot come into your life unless we make room by letting go of the old. How can plants bloom if the weeds are suffocating the roots? Many people lack the self-confidence and self esteem to make these transitions. What is self-esteem? Could this aspect of ourselves truly help us to have the strength to heal ourselves? In time, we will progress to this stage, but we have to start at the core of the problem first. It will take many centuries for society to get to a place where we can have such control of our destinies, but I would like to believe we could start the ball rolling with ourselves now, so our offspring can cultivate a high self-esteem society in the future.

There are so many aspects to developing high self-esteem and you may have some of them in place already. They just need to be refined and utilized to help develop the other areas that might not be so developed yet. Don't lose patience with yourself and understand that you are the important one to focus on and it will be as an awkward child taking that first ride on a bike. When you self esteem becomes stronger, so will your physical wellness. The rest of the world will begin to change around you little by little.

Chapter 19
Listen to Self Esteem

Does the ability to listen have anything to do with self-esteem? Yes, it does. Many of us think we are good listeners and some admit they don't really hear what is being said. The interpretation of perception of what we hear is based on several different factors.

How flexible you are with you listening abilities depends on the degree that you value judge what you hear. If you value judge most of the time, then you do not really hear what is being said because you already have a belief about that person or subject. The more you value judge, the lower you self esteem. If you have progressed at least to minimal judgment of others, you will find that you actually hear the other person much better. Your time is not spent thinking of ways to disagree or be better than the other person. If you are listening and you find yourself disagreeing, that is okay, but judging *them* for what they say and believe is not okay. You can ask questions to get clarification and allow them an opportunity to grow and expand by asking leading questions that may open up their "tunnel vision" or vice versa. As soon as one makes a statement, communication is closed. The other person may become insecure and invalidated that you are not really "hearing" them. Listening and hearing are not the same thing. People are normally open to a new thought if it isn't shoved down their throat. If it makes sense, even they will know it makes sense. That inner knower works with everyone.

I have developed myself over many years and the last 20 years it has been a conscious decision. The mentors in my life made such sense that I started learning voraciously. I have even thrown up after having a new realization about myself. I was in shock for a few days with an almost numb, low energy. I had an almost depressed feeling about myself like the life was drained from my body. This is actually a release of blocked energy, which is a good thing! I guess I had to *wear the new realization* for a while before I could face it and decide what to do with it.

The energy started to pick up again and I felt more liberated than before. It was like a weight lifted off my shoulders. If you do not understand you own needs, you will have difficulty expressing them in a way that someone will hear you. If you are wishy-washy about yourself, you will come across that way and people will stop listening. Your needs are always changing and identification of this, coupled with expression, will enable others to keep up with you or not. They still have choices just as you do.

There are many types of listening styles. Some people only like to listen to pleasurable things. They can daydream themselves right out of reality if the topic they are listening to is too detailed and uninteresting. They have difficulty staying in the present. Their eyes glaze over or they look down and doodle on paper. Ever see that "blank stare?" There is the person who can't follow the conversation unless they know the point of the conversation first. Once they know the core of the story they can process the rest of the data that supports the conclusion. If they come in on the middle of the story they have to ask what the topic is about before than can absorb. Another type is the person who can't hear because they can't take their eyes off the mustard on the speaker's tie or their hair is combed over their head. How many times do they have to refocus or ask for the story to be repeated?

There are the technical type listeners who hear only data and emotional types who can't hear the data because they are caught up in an emotional situation in another part of the room. There is a person who comes to a conclusion before the other person even finishes a thought. These types of listeners are always racing ahead and have to regroup when they realize the conversation wasn't going that direction. The point of discussing these various listening styles is to let you see how different we are even when we listen.

One is not better than another; it just is our predominant way to listen. You gravitate to your comfort zone because that is easy, but the goal is to be able to balance use of all the types. You listen differently and you accept information differently. You can't listen with your mouth open and you can't hear if you stay in one mode of listening. Everyone has a gift that can be of help to another. I certainly prefer not to go to a person who daydreams a lot when I need to learn to use a computer. I may want to daydream, but I have to adjust my style to hear the data. When I do get someone who can focus, understand they love their data and for a period of time, I had better love it if I want to use my computer with no help. Adjust to the person you are with while you are with them. If you just can't deal with it at the time, just say so. "I can't focus right now, maybe later." That is simple and you are being selfless by not wasting their time. When you are ready, this person will expand your knowledge and skills, help you to communicate better with others and allow you more independent flexibility in life. You will be showing respect to others and in turn, you will be more respected. You don't have to agree. A person with high self-esteem understands everyone and that is the goal: *To understand and not to judge.*

Chapter 20
Letting Go

So often people become disappointed with life, and/or situations, which seem to not bring the passion they seek. You still do not have control over others though you may feel you can "change them." Your expectation of the possibilities and potentials usually creates the disappointment. You may eventually develop an "I don't care attitude" to protect yourself from the pain that would normally ensue afterwards. The pain then gets stuffed down on top of other pains and the great wall starts going up to protect your fragile ego.

What is the answer? Always simple, but not easy. You are constantly evaluating your belief systems or should I say you need to re-evaluate your beliefs because nothing remains the same. When you hold on to people, memories or beliefs that are past you are only trying to fill a void for lack of any else to fill that void. You are disabling your growth and becoming stagnant. You get stuck inside those four walls and start spinning out of control. Your belief systems become outdated and so you continue to stand your ground for what your forefathers believed in and then can't understand why it isn't working for you now because the world has changed drastically.

What happened to the here and now and the new and improved beliefs which today's world seeks? You need to seek new ideals for yourself on an individual basis. Each person is unique and will have unique beliefs. You need to respect everyone's belief whether you agree or not. You become frustrated and angry, but continue to follow the same path because you are fearful of the unknown. It seems there was a time when people didn't have as much fear. The pioneers forged across the lands and had to accept death in many forms, but they continued. Now the average person can't walk to the store or get up to change the channel on the TV. Modern society has created such a small space to survive and find comfort. If the environment inside of your walls is not happy and peaceful, what can be expected when you find a window to air your life out? An instant breeze of relief and freedom.

Have any of you smelled anything stagnant or seen fungus, which grows on it? It is not attractive. That is what you are doing to yourselves by filling your voids with superficial stimuli. Instead of entertainment, it is a way of life. Dare forbid that you might go out and try something new and exciting! Blow the dust off as my mother would say!

I stated earlier that anger is a protective device for fear. People may be fearful of losing a good memory and create guilt for themselves if they add a new memory in exchange of loyalty for the old memory. They may feel so devoted to the memories because they feel that is what they are all about. Yes, that is a part of us, and at one time, those were new situations to us. When do we freeze frame our lives though? We get fixated on the value of someone or something and build up expectations only to find later that it is a long drop from the pedestal we placed them on. I have smacked on the bottom so many times and have been under what falls from the pedestal that I am surprised I still have my sanity. Positive memories are nice, but they soon need to find their place in the archives or we will stagnate and become complacent.

We also do the same thing with negative memories. We feel obligated to feel bad because that is what we believe is expected and what we know. Eventually those negative memories need to find their place in the archives and stop being the crutch for the rest of our lives. We cannot allow the past to dictate or control the present or the future and yet we utilize the future as a mirror of the past. That is when we get scared and hold on. It was said to me at one time that heaven is living in the present. Today. Not yesterday or tomorrow. I can't remember where I saw this saying but it certainly made sense to me.

Yesterday may have been hell and tomorrow is unknown, but today is what I make it. I have choice to do or not do anything. I can be angry or happy. I can't change the past, but I can choose for today to make tomorrow better.

I apologize for not being able to quote who said this. Maybe it was me! I am sure someone will contact me if it wasn't me! Learning to discern what to change depends on the results you are getting. You have heard the old saying, "If you keep doing what you are doing then you will keep getting what you are getting."

Are you able to see your patterns of behavior, which repeat themselves, or are you going to avoid the whole issue? It is your choice and you will create everything necessary to ensure that it happens as you believe it to be. What you believe, you will conceive and achieve. This is all a self-esteem issue.

We all know how miserable it feels when others hack at our self-esteem. If we feel the whack, we must not be too balanced. Knowing this is a beginning. Everyone, at one time, gets into a situation which erodes at our self-esteem. Knowing this will not allow it to get under the skin and rot us. We can say to ourselves that we are presently off balance and work toward regaining balance in quiet earnest. It all goes back to being honest with yourself and sizing up the true facts. If it isn't flowing with you at your speed, then you have to make a decision to create your balance. If others won't wait or can't keep up, you may have to make that new memory for yourself. Maybe the situation will re-connect at another time when the time is right for all. This is the time for you to let go and let God!

The expectations of "What ifs" will get you down every time if you don't take a chance. Letting go is difficult because you do not have the faith that your needs will be replenished in full and more abundantly. There is nothing wrong with attachment if it doesn't limit you. If you attach and stop where it feels safe, you will not feel the need to grow anymore. How many have said "All I wanted was a family, nice house and a nice car." When they got that, they became complacent in all aspects of life. They either took for granted or were being taken for granted. They gave up that dream of being a fashion designer or an architect.I have seen people work toward those hard to achieve goals even with a family, spouse-less or financially strapped. They make it because of the passion and commitment to achieve their dream.

They can't afford to be in a limiting attachment or they would never make it. You need energy coming in, not being drained out with a straw. Let go of the old if it isn't working and see what new comes in! You will find that your memories are not replaced, but can be a part of the new. Nothing is gone unless we choose it to be.

Chapter 21
Non Verbal Esteem

Everything I have been discussing to this point has involved feelings and emotions, which are expressed verbally. You have non-verbal ways to express your self-esteem. It has been identified that 35% of communication is verbal and 65% is nonverbal. There are variations of this percentage I am sure. So, if you increase the percentage of nonverbal communications to include the lack of ability, lack of skills or confidence to speak, there is an even larger percentage that becomes nonverbal and visual.

To sight a few examples of nonverbal cues: the effects of hair color/style, our dress, certain facial expressions or hand gestures. These can represent negative or positive attention. A hand wave could mean needing attention or being dismissed. Someone who asks you a question and then looks at their watch rather than giving you their undivided attention is a cue. Body posture, which turns away, is also a cue of nonverbal. Your perception may be different than what is meant to be conveyed and sometimes can be misread. Sometimes it is blatantly accurate. There are so many signals we take for granted, but we do need to pay attention to all of the aspects, as all are important in identifying a person's self esteem level.

I can identify a person's self esteem level through a handshake, the amount of eye contact I get from them or how "present" a person is when we are communicating. It usually goes without saying that confirmation of the level I may already perceive is granted by my diagnosis of the nonverbal cues they have already given me. I can sit back in a group of people and observe others in communication mode and identify their level of self-esteem without them knowing. It is very interesting to do, but you have to have high self-esteem to do it. You have to be able to feel secure with yourself and know the signs of insecurity.

I have also discussed how perception of ourselves has been developed by those who have trained us and that perception relies on how they saw themselves. Is it distorted or normal? Your self-image is the root of your visual observable behavior. It is different than your self-esteem. Your self-image is what you want others to see visually. Your self-esteem is what you feel about you. Your image can be the color of your skin, odors, hair, eyes, teeth, clothing styles, the car your drive or the house you live in. Clothing alone can identify how a person is feeling or wants to be identified. It can attract others, be a group identification, a protectiveness or status. I have met many people who have used clothing as a means to hide or confuse others as to their own real identity. All can be used to manipulate or to persuade others. *All that glitters is not always real gold!* Of course, your level of self-esteem will determine whether something is for the good or reaching toward a goal in an appropriate fashion. Take a look at yourself when you leave the house. What do you want people to perceive you to be? There are times I have dressed sloppy so people will leave me alone when I go out. I may not feel like talking or even being noticed.

Your voice is also a clue as to your level of self-esteem. The tone, pitch, intensity are all factors. Shy people talk so softly you can barely hear them. Too loud can also be a front for low self esteem and is used to intimidate. The way you tilt your head, lift a brow, contort your lips or any gestural body movements are actual attitudes about the situation you are in. Your body movements can tell others how open to receiving them you are or how closed or judgmental you are going to be with them.

Tactile communication is the most basic form and is used by humans and animals. It is the first sensory stimulus developed with babies. If there is lack of touching as a child, it will be more difficult to develop, as you get older. It can still be relearned if it is distorted. You need to know what is distorted to change it. Touch is the most basic and yet the most crucial aspect between partners.

All of the factors described in this chapter have an effect on your attitude and your attitude has an effect on how you communicate yourself to others. Do you walk around with your head down and no eye contact? Do you isolate from everyone because you are fearful of interaction? Do you have a scowl on your face most of the time? Do you judge others and are you being judged? Have you noticed I have not communicated about any verbal communication and I bet you can relate to everything I have written? I bet you have been able to picture yourself in a multitude of nonverbal behavioral trends. The problem is most people don't pay attention in a conscious manner. We take it all for granted. Most people are too busy worrying about the verbal message. How often have you been in a situation where the words and actions do not coincide? I was in several relationships that worked this way. Did I pay attention? No, not at first. But after time and repeated conditions, I could see the pattern and started to pay more attention to the action versus words.

The verbal message rarely tells the story without some major digging and then the people have to be open and trusting. The smallest change in gestures or body movements can alter what is observed and perceived. It then affects our emotions instantaneously. If you have low self-esteem, it will affect you with a much greater intensity. The higher your self-esteem, the less others will affect you and the less you will be manipulated by others. You will begin to have more control of yourself when you truly look at what others see and the affect it has on them. In return, it will affect you as well by their response to you. The choice is always yours. As always.

Chapter 22
Self Esteem

I have discussed all of the different aspects that make up self-esteem and the aspects that influence self esteem. I have also discussed what self-esteem can create for you. Low self-esteem is the cause of one's individual and social problems. It is the lack of love and understanding of our present identity and the inability to accept this identity in an unconditional manner. Many people allow their own mistakes and failures to dictate the way they feel about themselves and then allow others to dictate their opinions on to us which magnifies and layers our own self-guilt. This leads to unhealthy attitudes and causes a chain reaction of negative emotions, which permeates into all of society. It affects the balance of energy that makes miracles happen.

Good things can happen to us despite ourselves and I can attest to that personally. I have been caught in the middle of more chaos in my life and did not know how I got there. All of a sudden, I was in it and no sign of relief and no tools to escape that I was aware. I realize, now, that it was a test of faith and a learning experience for me even though, at the time, I was blind to any reason I deserved this "lack of things" more than once in my life. Lo and behold, out of the clouds came a helping hand and provided me with the money or tools to help me out of the situation. My mother was a huge support for me and surprisingly so, as I expected she would be the first to nail me with all of the should, ought's and musts that I needed to do. Come to think of it she did give me her "food for thought", but after many battles of will, she did refrain from too much criticism and let me fumble through finally. Strangers, some old friends and some new acquaintances gave me my tools. The common comment I heard from all was, that at one time, someone had helped them up and they wanted to return the favor to someone in need. I learned humbleness and what it really meant. I learned to appreciate all things and not to take anything for granted as it can be taken away as easily as it is given without gratitude.

I reached a point of not having a car, a job or money. I managed to keep a roof over my head, but it was a big struggle to not give up. One month, I had to have a yard sale to make my rent. I remembered that if you let go of the old things that new would be replacing them eventually. So I wasn't too upset about giving the things up. And yes, Mother, I still have the family heirlooms.

The point I want to make clear is the helping hand came, but it did not provide all. I had to take the reins and follow through with action on my part to correct the situations whether I created the situation or not. I can see that I played a part in the creation by allowing others' activities to affect my life as I was standing in a state of "love" and "loyalty" as a friend. The pile came down on me at once as they skirted away before it hit them. Since I was brought up to accept the consequences and the responsibility to make amends and survive, my "friends" would disappear until I got the mess straightened out and then what do you know, here they came again! How many red flags did it take for me to realize that I had better be my own best friend because I knew I would not let me down? My self-esteem was damaged, but I was able to recuperate quickly because I had been taught to cope. I knew the next journey was for myself and the next people in my life would not interfere because I choose to be with people that have like thinking.

So, do you get the picture of self-esteem a little better? If you learn to count on you, and make the changes necessary to make yourself strong, you will act, speak and think differently with positive results. It will permeate back into society and start sprouting buds of peace, happiness and contentment that we are all craving. You will be able to love and be loved as God planned. The tools are out there and you possess the ability to think and make choices, which are the biggest tools to have always. If you truly want to get on the path to stabilize a positive physical, mental and emotional well being for yourself, you need to start now. Just reading this book is a start.

You have to educate yourself and fill your mind with new information and reading is the best way to start and inexpensive as well. You can attend seminars and probably find things on the computer now. You can be around positive people who can help you become more aware. Peer enlightenment is a good healer if the people have high esteem. They will nurture you through it in a non-threatening manner without making you feel less than a person.

Self-esteem involves many aspects of our being. It is your emotions, feelings, perceptions, expressions and communications, verbal and nonverbal, your beliefs, values, attitudes, listening abilities and choices we make. It is how you love, how you trust, how you handle conflict, how you set limits and boundaries for yourself, how you take care of your body, the amount and degree of risk you take, the degree of commitment and follow through you have and how honest you can be with yourself and others. And most of all, it is how accepting you are of yourself and others.

If your needs outweigh your desires and wants, your expectations of yourself and others are unrealistic and judging, everything out of your mouth is negative, opinionated or guilt causing, then you can safely assume you are out of alignment with a healthy self esteem. If you are always bored or lonely, wearing masks, fearful, angry, anxious, hurting, depressed, isolating, and experiencing more consequence than reward, you can also safely assume you are out of alignment with a healthy self esteem. Inability to communicate needs or beliefs is also a sign of an undeveloped self-esteem. I say undeveloped because it can be developed. Developed and undeveloped are high self-esteem words. Low self-esteem words are good/bad, or strong/weak. The high self-esteem words allow room for growth in a non-threatening manner.

Mistakes and failures are good. They direct us. They teach us. They allow us to increase our self-awareness as well as the informational input you get from books or seminars. The balance of positive and negative input into your life will help balance and heal your soul. When the two are out of balance, you experience negative results through fear, anger, hurtful tones and actions. Remember, for every one-minute of negative input, it takes ten minutes of positive input to counteract and heal. Think of the entire negative input received through the media and other unhappy people on a daily basis and then figure out how long it will take to heal the world. It is monumental the way we are going. So, instead of trying to change the world, we each need only to work on the outcome of ourselves and the world will begin to change. It has to start with you. You. You. You. Responsibility to yourself. You need faith and the hope that what you ask for to assist you on your journey will be provided even if it is one moment of peace and silence to hear yourself think

.

Listen to some soothing music without words to allow your mind to embrace the peace. As I write this book, I have a CD, which includes Mozart, Pachebel, Tchaikovsky, Dvork, Schubert, Beethoven and others. I feel I am inspired by the greatness of their gifts and that it will help open up my mind to allow my gift to come through in a positive flow of thought. It works for me. You need to find what gives you peace and take the time each day to reflect. You will be astounded by the peace that comes from quieting the mind.

Chapter 23
Coping Levels

Everyone has self-esteem. Everyone has some self-awareness. The question is what level have we developed? We are uniquely at the level we are supposed to be at this time. Some people do not know how to handle success and some people do not know how to be happy. Either way, a path is designated for growth to reach our own balance with the goal being peace of mind. The key to reaching this goal is coping skills. If blessings are coming your way, do you know how to handle it? If blessings are hidden, do you know how to find them?

Reality is...there will always be turbulent times. These times of crisis and peril actually allow us time for introspection of our belief systems. You have been given the gift and right to choose your path. You can choose a higher path or a lower path. The intensity of what you believe and value most at the time will dominate the direction you will take. The wondrous thing is you can always choose another path if you feel you made the wrong choice.

Your self esteem needs to be fed and nurtured daily to enable your coping skills the strength to work. If you are too tired, problems seem more exaggerated and overwhelming. Your ability to cope becomes vulnerable. As your body needs nurtured and fed daily, so does your mind and spirit. We have so much negativity hitting us daily. We barely have time to nurture ourselves unless we take time to have some peace at home. If there is no peace at home then we are fighting a losing battle. Your home should be your castle and I don't refer to everyone being a slave to you. I mean it should be a place to feel safe and secure and loved.

What is coping? The dictionary says coping is how you deal with problems and troubles. *It also means to match equally.* You do have to match energy, equally, to cope effectively. The one-minute of negative input has to be equally matched by the IO minutes of positive input or the negative rules. The battle can be won with the appropriate weapons and tools, which you have to learn and practice daily. It is wonderful to have the knowledge, but if you do not put it into action, the knowledge is useless.

You have to change your words and your way of thinking to a more productive and positive tone. Listen to yourself. How often do you say, "Can't, shouldn't, ought to, must?" Are you constantly criticizing everything and everybody? Do you justify your position of the present? Are you coping or have you given up and are now letting life control you? You can have high self-esteem and experience a trauma one day and slide right back into a state of fear or depression. If you have a healthy base, you are less likely to stay in that state for long. You will experience the normal stages of grief on a realistic time frame and then pull yourself back up more quickly. Again, the degree of the trauma or problem will be the degree of healing needed. A death of a loved one could take a lot longer to heal whereas a bounced check would take a minimal amount of time to heal. Letting go and accepting *"what is"* as part of life's constant change and realizing that it is necessary to experience the grief is a very difficult aspect for people to remember and practice.

Most of us forget to treat ourselves as children when we get a booboo. Remember the drama as a child when something horrific happened like scraping your knee. You probably let out a scream as if you had broken every bone in your body. Your parents didn't even want to look at first for fear of the worst. Through appropriate nurturing from the adults in your life you would begin to relax and accept that even your own worst fear wasn't nearly as bad as you thought. You may have stared at your knee, perhaps every day, but it became less scary and you continued your daily routines as it healed. If the nurturing hadn't happened, you would not have learned to control the drama and see what is actually wrong. That is how many adults handle stress. They dramatize the situation because they do not want to see what is actually wrong. People who did not get any nurturing feel "less than" for having scraped their knee. They did not get permission to feel the pain, so they stuff pain. "How could you have done that? You shouldn't have been playing on the banister" they might say to a child. *OK...maybe that is all true, but I have some pain here...can we focus on that, so I can move on.*

This is where coping skills or lack of coping skills begin; making a child feel bad for a normal childhood accident is not teaching them to cope in a positive light and sets the stage for the beginning of low self esteem. They cannot see that life has its normal expectant happenings, good and bad. Children have accidents. That is a fact. Children are explorers, navigators, and risk takers and are thirsty for truth. Why punish them for finding the truth? Maybe that is why we are afraid to seek the truth. We will be considered bad! Boy, do we have a lot to undo!

As an adult, we commit an adult booboo and depending on how we were conditioned to respond as a child is how we respond as an adult. We will have patience and positive self-talk if nurtured properly. We will use positive affirmations like "I have to make this work." If on the other hand, you were yelled at, your self talk may go something like, "I should not have been doing this, it is my fault." You will kick yourself down the sidewalk and usually take it out on others along the way.

Realize people make mistakes, encounter problems and obstacles that are equal to our mental and social development. To match *equally* is coping on our own level of development. Level of development can be seen in the attitudes of people and the behavior they exhibit daily. If you still act like a child, then you will cope as a child in the manner you were conditioned. Until you begin to expand your skill to cope, and it is a skill, you will remain in your fuddle of negative bliss. A skill is learned. The more you do it the better you become. You need to learn appropriate ways and then practice it.

More than likely, you are reaching adulthood or already there. You will undoubtedly have to reprogram and re-educate yourself because most people are in the same boat. Up a creek without that paddle. Be open to watch and observe a truly grounded person. If there are none around, books are very safe. The skill of identifying a person who is really grounded isn't easy. There are many masks to look behind. Someone who is at peace with their life will permeate peace and understanding and you will feel it. Your inner knower will know. These people will not cause pain maliciously. Truth can sometimes be interpreted as a pain infliction so the tone of voice and manner of delivery must be taken into account as well. Do you see how all of the aspects I have talked about come into play to help you make wiser choices?

This whole process will take work and it will feel awkward like the child trying to stay up on that two wheel bike for the first time. What better project than yourself? You have the rest of your life to reach a goal, the goal of self-satisfaction or actualization. Many people are striving for the wrong goals first. Money comes and goes, your friends come and go and even your family can come and go. You are always with you. Learn to nurture yourself as a child and give yourself the permission to grieve and make mistakes. Obstacles will always be there. As you become more skilled at coping, you will begin to soar over problems with unencumbered speed and tranquility. The final ingredients are faith, trust and hope. This is the spiritual side of yourself.

A study was done at Harvard a while ago. The results showed that the majority of people spent the highest percentage of their time striving toward power, influence and material possessions. One percent of their time was spent on developing themselves. If they reversed these percentages and placed development of self at the top, the rest of their goals would fall into place with ease. Instead, they choose to struggle against their natural flow to achieve their goals because they do not know what is their natural flow.

☙❧

Chapter 24
What to Expect

In order to start your new adventure, you have to be ready for it. You have to be like a child again and be thirsty for the truth. You have to be able to take risks and face some realities different than what you have learned. You have to know that you are the most important person right now. This may sound selfish and to some degree it is. You are the number one priority. This does not mean you trample over others, manipulate or intimidate them or become a complete hermit with no social life at all. Remember the children who look at their scraped knees daily but they continue on.

There will be times when you feel all alone and there will be times when you will be thankful to be alone. You will get confused, frustrated, shocked, angry, scared and eventually enlightenment will come. You will feel, at times, there is no light at the end of the tunnel. You will give up more than once and you will fall down more than once. Sometimes you will need to rest your mind by not thinking at all until your strength comes back.

The reprogramming means either erasing what does not work or adjusting your present ways of thinking to change the activity. Are you getting results for what you want or for what others want for you? This can be difficult to discern because some have had many years of coaching and are listening to old tapes that have played over and over. Some still have the same coaches still trying to coach.

We have learned to cope in some form, but not all in productive ways. Some people drink, do drugs, eat improperly or become promiscuous to avoid truth.

We seek out that which we did not get growing up. If we did not get comfort and nurturing we seek it out in the manner we were taught to nurture. Abuse can be considered nurturing to some if that is what their reality dictated, therefore they will seek out abuse. Distorted ways breed distorted needs and desires. So one needs to know what is true comfort and nurturing. We start to cope as soon as we wake up in the morning and are conscious. Our attitude directs our choices. We are all pushed to the extremes when we can't stretch anymore. We blame others when we can't see the origin of our problems. Some choose not to cope because they get complacent or just give up. Society feels sorry for them and enables their inability to cope by giving to them instead of teaching them to fish.

There comes a point when one needs to be taught to fish. Some people have been conditioned to freely take what others have, but when anything is taken away from them, they whimper and complain. This has become a spoiled society. When something of importance to them is taken away, they wake up for awhile out of fear. They struggle to regain what is gone and when they get it they fall back into baseline behavior again. They never contemplated they actually found the energy to fight for what was lost. They just fall back into complacency not remembering the strength came from somewhere. They learned nothing.

An open mind and heart is your best teacher. Every moment of your life is a time to learn every person you come into contact with has something to teach you. Sometimes this can hurt, but it is a part of the growth. Learning never ends. Self-sacrifice is not expected to be painless. If you have the desire for something out of reach, the pain is joyous in the struggle. I am a firm believer that a good relationship will not take that much work. It should be easy. If both people know themselves and can express that up front, there will be no surprises or conflict. The flow will be smooth. The right job will not be a chore, but a challenge. The contentment of the job will be its reward. Ninety percent of the populations are in jobs they don't like.

We keep going along hoping we will harvest the fruits of our labor and if this doesn't happen immediately we cope by retreating, leaving, hurting others or creating another problem to take the place of the one you don't want to face. It all builds up only to come tumbling down. If you can be honest with yourself, how you feel and what you want, the direction is there for you. You will know what to do.

Why do you think they call the age of forty the mid-life crisis? This is the age we usually wake up. We wonder where we have been and what we have been doing. We ponder what needs to be changed and some take the risk to change it. I have seen some start a whole new life with a new job, partner and a new way of thinking. They realize that the second part of like is a second chance to live happily with the knowledge that has been collected. Others think it but stay stuck in the past. They put up with and hold on to what might have been. If it were meant to be, it would be. If it is time to grow and move on, then move on. Accept the responsibility for what you are leaving because you helped create it. Take the first step into the future with a fresh and enlightened outlook. If you did not learn any lessons, your path will repeat itself until you do. The grass is only greener on the other side if you learned how to keep it that way.

People's growth accelerates by the gifts we give each other along the way and the lessons learned. When we reach a no growth point it is time to move on. You are still seeking your own level of understanding. If a relationship has reached a point of stagnation, let it go. Do not become the stagnant essence and deny yourself the possibility of future lessons and gifts that help you achieve who ultimately you are to become. When you have had enough pain, it is time to go. If you are in a relationship and still love each other you will find a way to make it work.

Chapter 25
Disappointment & Grief

I have discussed different emotions, the purpose for them and what happens if you deny them. I have discussed how they affect you physically and how your body is the road map to the way you live your life. The problems that face you on a daily basis can produce disappointment. Your past can create disappointment. All have experienced disappointment. Many may or may have not learned to cope with disappointment? How you do this has a great effect on your self-esteem in the end. It is not easy since it has become a routine habit to cope in the same way each time if we choose to change nothing. If it becomes unfinished business for you and halts your growth, you probably do not understand the natural grieving process and where you might be stuck.

Some have experienced more grandiose situations than others, but bottom line for all is we all perceive our story to be unique. That is until we hear someone else's story. The test is whether you commiserate with them or rise above and look for solutions. There is a solution to every problem. This is what separates people. Some accept that their path cannot change and others will not accept the path and seek to find the answer. What directs you is the perception from your past conditioning. You can change your life! You have to be the one to change it. No one else can do it. Others can guide you, but ultimately, the call is yours.

As I have said before, your attitude plays an important role. If you have a bad attitude about life and you know you do, that is at least realistic and honest. This is your reality as you know it. It hurts so much that you cannot anticipate it any other way. If you choose not to change it and you are comfortable with that, then you need to accept all things that go with it. You can't change the past, but you can change the future. The future is your choice. The past was not your reality, however distorted, but was someone else's reality that was given to you when you were trying to learn and understand life. I am sure it seems too overwhelming to even bother, right? Some people can be comfortable being uncomfortable. Yes, that is a reality also.

I feel you need to understand the grief process that all humans experience for even the smallest disappointment. Some of you may be stuck in one of the stages of grieving and can't find your way out. The grieving process is simple, but of course, not easy. Like anything else, you need to understand what the process is in order to evaluate where you are stuck. My purpose is to expand your awareness of things to help you find your tools for growth. You could be stuck in the second step or the first step. Obviously, you have not made it to the last step because you have not let go of an issue that is still holding you back.

You cannot allow the new to come in if you choose to keep all of the old. Are you a pack rat of the past? You have to make a conscious effort to keep moving forward at times when it seems the most difficult. I had to put my dog to sleep recently. We were one. He knew my moods so well, my humor and my fears. He protected me without violence and loved me when I needed it the most. To say the least, it was a trauma for me. A friend of mine, a psychologist in San Diego, Dr. Kent Layton, must have known how troubled I was and immediately began to help me through the process of grief. He gave me money to go out to dinner and expected me to use it for that. He suggested I change or rearrange my furniture; buy new things that I couldn't have when I had the dog. He said "Create the change!" I did all of the things he told me even though I didn't feel like it. Looking back, what help that was to me. I felt myself wanting to hold on longer, but knew reality was that he was gone and not coming back. I had a choice and knew that if I didn't follow through with the changes, I would have been stuck for a lot longer than I wanted.

I had to keep moving and changing to make room for the new things in my path. It was over a year and I still have memories, but the pain diminished daily and I have accomplished quite a bit in place of the void. I created an environment that I knew I really wanted and I figure the time was now. It takes time depending on what the level of grief may be. Overcoming the guilt of feeling disloyal or disrespectful to the memory of a lost attachment is probably one of the most difficult things to do. It took at least 2 years for me to feel I had passed into the acceptance phase.

Either way, whether it was a positive or negative experience, you have placed a certain loyalty and respect on the issue. Based on your present reality it is difficult to overcome the guilt of letting go. You have to displace yourself. You need to say, "I am with myself now and whatever memory I am having difficulty letting go of and or whatever is triggering the grief aspects in me, I need to change and change now." One of my other mentors gave me a mantra to say as many times as I needed to begin reprogramming my thinking. It is, "That was then, this is now and everything has changed." He said for me to say it a hundred times in a minute if the grief was really powerful. After you say it you can go back to the memory, but continue saying it until the feelings become less powerful. This is when you know the reprogramming is beginning to work.

If you can truly absorb, understand and process the following steps of grief, you will conquer one of your biggest hurdles. These steps apply to all levels of disappointment. Disappointment can merely be a situation that you can't fit into your clothes in the morning or it can escalate to a higher level because a relationship ends by death or circumstance. It can be a problem with your weight or lack of weight. The result of disappointment, anger, guilt and depression still fall into a grieving process. For whatever the situation, if there are negative emotions or the "sting" is still there, you are still stuck in one of the stages. This has a great effect on a person's self esteem because it inhibits more growth of the soul. It is a block that needs unblocking.

The same psychologist I know deals with trauma cases that far exceed what our imaginations could ever create in the worst horror flick. He has to deal with the grieving processes of those who have no hope left. I have discussed this process and how he uses it to educate his patients. I have been aware of the process for a long time, and did not realize how difficult it really is for people to get though all of the stages and to let go of what they get fixated on. I want you to feel your way through, not think your way through the following paragraphs. Choose a situation that is already past and accepted so you can recognize each step as we go through them.

STEP ONE:
Shock: This step speaks for itself. I believe we have all experienced and felt shock. There is no room for emotion here because every part of you seems to come to a stop. Your mind and body jolts to a freeze frame. Shock can last from 15 minutes to 3 days or longer. You feel numb; you attempt to touch base with reality and try to find the correct emotion to protect you. You try to decide what has happened. Depending on the degree of shock, you will experience an equal reaction time and response.

Say your spouse has said he/she wants a divorce. You had no idea. You are shocked and can't decide what to feel. You become speechless and just stare vacantly. Your ability to cope with this situation, rationally, is directly related to your self-esteem level. In other words, how you have been taught to cope with disappointment will depend on the level of self-esteem of the people that surrounded you in your learning years. You will mimic their response. The degree of shock will become less as you develop more in awareness of yourself and develop better coping skills for the unknown. Shock exists and no one is exempt from it. The unknown is what shocks you. If it is a situation that repeats itself, the shock value diminishes with repeated occurrence. The first experience is the worst.

STEP TWO:
Disbelief: Again, anyone can feel what disbelief conjures up in us. You repeat over and over, "I can't believe this is happening, or I can't believe you said that." The key phrase

is *can't believe*. When you hear yourself repeating these statements in some form, you are in the disbelief stage. You try to get clarification by asking "What do you mean?" or "Why are you doing this?" It usually comes in question form. "Are you saying you don't love me anymore and you want a divorce?" You are still trying to control your outburst of emotion at this time until you are clear. Very Clear! Then watch...the emotions are like a flood that came from nowhere.

STEP THREE:
Denial: This stage is the biggest step to get out safely. You could stay in this stage forever if you're not careful and some people do. Some people may even make up a false scenario just to get them through the pain or rather avoid the extreme pain. Many people justify, blame, make excuses, and look for solutions along the wrong path. Many people feel guilt; turn the situation back and forth between yourself and someone else, regarding whose fault. You may create more problems for yourself at times to comfort yourself from the pain. This is when you drink, do drugs, shoplift or whatever your choice of escape may be. You may try to pull others into the situation. You may become physically ill. The longer you are in denial, the worse the problem or illness gets.

Illness starts in the spirit first and then turns into the physical. The stress denies energy to a certain part of your body and it gets weak. Illness is somatic and symptomatic of what you conscious does not want to accept. Any denial is expressed physically. Illness and behavioral issues relate to your specific past and what you have come to believe and value. If you believe in your illness and have come to value it as an excuse for your problems, you are still in denial.

Many people spend all of their lives talking about what they can't do. They still have the sting of negative emotion when they think of the person or situation that "put them in this position." The more powerful the sting, the more you are denying and the bigger the problems become. When the sting of negative emotion disappears, you are progressing forward into the next steps.

STEP FOUR:

Searching: You begin to look for answers that will help you to hold on to the memory of a person or situation. You might create shrines by leaving pictures out or leaving a room intact the way it was when the person was still around. You may make a conscious effort to halt change as much as possible. You could become engrossed in memories to the point of it overtaking your day. Songs may trigger a memory or visiting a place that an occurrence took place. Whether it was a positive or negative memory, you will create the feelings appropriate to the situation when triggered. You may become loyal to the memory because you believe it is part of you forever in that form only.

You might search for all of the things you could have done to change the outcome. "If I would have done this," or "if he/she would not have done that." If you are in denial and searching for a way to repair a situation that is definitely ended, you will eventually become depressed or bitter, because the actual solution is to let go, not hold on. People continue to hold on and then they start to beat up on themselves or others. "What is wrong with me?" "What did I do wrong?" That is a question that can bury you or help you find solutions depending on your attitude and self-esteem. Sometimes it is not your issue at all, but you have created the need to hold on because you may not have had a life of your own. Sometimes you are in someone else's space when they are dealing with their own issues and you become the target and allow yourself to be put upon. You can also have a different attitude and learn from it no matter what occurred.

Each situation or person is an opportunity for you to look at yourself. You can accept that maybe you need to change some areas or you can grovel in guilt over what might have been. If you can accept each situation in your life as a gift, you will be able to go through the grieving process much more smoothly. Stop searching and deal with what is reality.

STEP FIVE:

Bargaining: You may start to bargain with yourself and others. Usually one bargains with God because you feel he is the only one with the power. The less effort you put into this is all right with you. You make promises you may or may not keep, depending on your insight to the situation. When you don't keep your promise you kick yourself until *you become sick and tired of being sick and tired*. Then you can choose to make a commitment to change things and stick with it or not.

Life is not a bargaining table. It is to gain insight into all that happens so you can make the necessary changes for a better quality of life. How many times do you make New Year's resolutions and break them the next morning? Guilt sets in and subconsciously you add another layer, which weighs down the ability to be fully happy. You look back silently with inner grief at yourself. You need to stay focused and committed to do it for yourself. God will give you the strength and a path to follow if you listen and watch, but we are a stubborn breed! We don't listen.

If your insight is healthy and honest and you make the commitment to change, you will only do what you would rather do than not do. You are ready to let go and accept.

STEP SIX:

Acceptance: If you made it to acceptance, reality has finally reached a balance for you about the grieved issue. You accept the situation and the sting is gone. Or so you think. At times you may slide back and forth through all of the steps several times before you truly accept and move on. Your progress starts slowly and there will be triggers that could set you back for awhile.

The occurrences should be more rapid with less impact each time. You can start to doubt your acceptance and experience the same feeling but your strength will begin to pull you through. You may even begin to crave the situation in times of loneliness or boredom and if the opportunity arises you may even attempt to jump back into the frying pan again to see if maybe you were wrong or your insight was not clear enough.

Acceptance is when you can move on with a confident air and no doubt. The past is past. You can remove the shrines in your mind and/or in your house. You can stand absolutely sure that you will be all right and better for having made it through. You have processed in a healthy manner and are healed. Give yourself time to heal. You may be impatient and want it to be all right now and yesterday. Some people are sometimes embarrassed if they don't flow smoothly through this. You may even act like everything is all right when it isn't. Your self-esteem level depends on the amount of time you spend becoming aware of yourself and what it takes to make you strong. Positive strengthens and negative weakens.

Remember, we are bombarded daily with negativity and it takes much conscious positive input to overcome it. There will be few who will truly help you get to that point, but rely on yourself first.

I would like to add my own steps to the grieving process. *Commitment and Action,* you have to make a conscious effort to do this. You have to force yourself at times to make the changes work. Create a small goal daily, until it becomes a part of your new nature. It will feel awkward and uncomfortable, but you will be surprised after the first step, it becomes easier. You have to take the first step. Do not sit and think about it and hope it works out because you bargained for it to happen that way. Use positive affirmations and confident words. I will make this happen. You and your self-esteem will be the better for it.

Chapter 26
Obstacles and Esteem

Obstacles are a reality we cannot escape. They can pop up at any time and do. They are what help us grow to a higher level. Someone with high self-esteem will take a deep breath and say here we go. It is a very organized, methodical thought process. You begin by discerning what you have control over and what you don't have control over. What you do not have control over you dismiss. You concentrate on what you do have control over. It is a test of confidence, endurance and maintaining balance until the solution surfaces. It is also having faith in your ability to make choices and believing in what you feel is correct for you.

The great leaders of time have achieved the knowledge of self, their limitations and their strengths. They surround themselves with people who can do the things they prefer not to do or someone who has ability the leader has not developed. They know the puzzle of life includes utilizing the strengths of everyone to create a powerful outcome. It is a team effort. A leader has the ability to see the strengths of others and they do not have a battle of egos. They alleviate their stress by finding people who also know themselves and function in a similar capacity of knowing their developed and undeveloped areas. When everyone knows their expertise, they do not need to carry facades and they trust the other person's abilities. If you carry a façade, the hidden undeveloped areas will be exposed, the trust level diminishes and production falls short.

This follows the same path in relationships, jobs, friend-ships and world interaction. We need to be aware of each other and what the person can contribute. No one can be all things to all people and should not be expected to be all things.

When obstacles arise in relationships, it can be an all out war if both people become temporarily blinded by the shock of indifference. Two low self-esteem people will destroy each other beyond repair because they will lose rational and bal-anced thinking abilities on how to solve a situation utilizing the strengths of each other. They cannot see the strengths of the other, so they blame and value judge each other until hate becomes paramount. Bitterness sets in and nothing gets ac-complished. It may be time to accept that the relationship has met its level of growth for both and isn't benefitting anyone anymore. If growth and new awareness does not occur, they will seek out another low self-esteem person to commiserate with them. It is a continued cycle until growth occurs with one or both people.

One high self esteem person and one low self-esteem person has a slightly better chance if the low self esteem per is honest that they do not know what to do. They ask for help and are willing to go the mile. The high self-esteem person will give that person space and guidance by being the wind beneath their wings. They will provide the environment con-ducive to growth as long as they see the effort is sincere. They can be the teacher by example or direct them to people who have no emotional ties and yet provide a safe and trusting en-vironment for growth. If the low self esteem person is needy and has no intention of growing and changing and expects the high self esteem person to handle everything, it will eventu-ally suck the life out of the high self esteem person. The low self-esteem person will nag and berate their companion and the battle begins. The original obstacle now blows up into multiple obstacles and the illusions of love are eliminated. The high esteem person will begin to withdraw and try to get re-balanced while the low self-esteem seeks out allies to justify their position. In the end, it does no good. Each will go their own way seeking out another on the level they choose to be on.

Two high self esteem people have needs, but are not needy. They can accept the faults of the other because they are able to make a wise choice in the beginning. They are free of illusions. They are able to tell the other who they are and what they expect. They were able to see the person for who they are because their intention is not to hide behind or be in front of, but to walk equally and individually. They want peace and a working relationship where both can thrive in being themselves without retribution and judgment. No one is destroyed or damaged. The energy flows well and the obstacles are handled in a rational manner. They can decide at any point that it is time to move on, but if the love is there, they will stay on the same path.

Everyone is on their own level of growth with their self-esteem and no two people will ever be on the same level. That is what makes life interesting. We learn from each other if we can be honest with ourselves about what is happening. I feel the closer two people are with their self-esteem levels, the greater the chance of success in the relationship. Combine that with love, passion and respect and you achieve heaven on earth. You will be able to love because you love yourself.

Countries at war are merely people at war. Take a look at the different countries and try to distinguish which ones have high/low self esteem. I feel the USA has high self esteem on the whole as a country, but there are many short circuits in the makeup of the whole. We try to help the other countries but some don't want our help and are not ready to accept that they have strengths other than to fight. They continue to split facets instead of trying to pull together and create a powerful world of respect and distinction. We need to understand that other countries have gifts and strengths to offer and we are not the only ones who exist. Too much of a good thing does not give anyone the right to control or demean another. We do our best and growth continues.

We have it so good in this country and most of the citizens do not even realize it. We just sit back in our easy chairs and judge the world. Look at yourself when judging and see how you like it! I have lived in another country and experienced their gifts, their limitations, their history, which they also are very proud to display. I am thankful even more to be an American, but I do not discount that the world as a whole is a part of us as a whole. Whether it is two people or two thousand people, the results are achieved the same way. Understand, respect and appreciate those for who they are and what they too can achieve for the whole.

I hope you do not feel I am off the track because I am trying to help you see how powerful high self esteem can be and how much low self-esteem destroys. Whether it is you, a relationship or world peace, there is a need to start becoming the powerful person that does exist, but is temporarily hidden by the chatter of negative input. It has to start with yourself and then you can begin to help lift others in an appropriate and high self esteem fashion. Allow the energies to flow in a productive mode rather than destructive mode.

Chapter 27
What is Self Esteem?

Up to this point, I have tried to dissect every part of your emotions that I feel you may misunderstand, be confused about or simply have no awareness of at all. I have tried to explain to you that you can be as normal as you wish and with the wisdom I have learned, hopefully will help you understand where you are and what is actually happening to you.

My purpose is to help you be open to learning and increase your awareness of yourself. In turn, this will help you to let go of fear, stress and decrease the unknown factor, which causes frustration and depression. The more you protect your faults without facing them, the more you will experience the non-motivating mental issues that keep you down. The more you know about yourself, the less doubt you have about the choices you need to make for yourself. People will not be able to pull you in different directions other than the one you need to be going. Your own direction.

Developing high self-esteem is learned, just like learning to read. You may notice I repeat concepts over and over so it sticks in your mind better. Some of us have had many teachers through life experiences and a few have made a great impact that helped pave our road. Some were pleasurable and some not so pleasurable. Both were placed there for us to learn. Socrates said many moons ago "Know thyself and to thine own self be true!" Where did he learn this concept? This is obviously a very old issue that people have dealt with over time. People lead and people follow. How many true leaders can you say have emerged out of the infinite number of people that have existed? The percentage is fewer than greater. I believe that everyone could say that a great leader is compassionate, fair, honest and trustworthy. They had to learn lessons like everyone else. The difference is they had a thirst to know what "better" really means. Their self esteem had reached a peaceful and contented level where they could focus their attentions on others without it affecting their own balance. They could give of themselves because they were fulfilled by self, not material possessions and other external gratifications.

Self esteem is making informed decisions for yourself and trusting your intuition to help direct you through the rough spots when you do not have all the information. Self-esteem is not being afraid to try something new whether it works out or not and getting up and going for it again. Self-esteem is standing up for what you believe and allowing others to do the same in a calm and rational manner. Self-esteem knows that you are not perfect and failures are part of the perfection process. Self-esteem understands that every emotion, every situation and every interaction is part of our growth. Self esteem is feeling good that you have done your best to the present based on the knowledge you had at the time. If your awareness was different, your actions may have been different. It knows you know and accepting when you don't know. It is being kind to yourself as you would be to a best friend. It is finding your balance, adjusting your developed and undeveloped areas so they work in harmony. Self esteem is being able to say, "I like myself and what I am becoming. Everything I have been through has made me who I am!"

You may see pain and happiness through a tunnel of past human awareness and therefore may find it difficult to believe you can live without being in denial about yourself and your future. When you can enjoy the journey and mystery of growth, knowing that it will lead you to what you seek with minimal growing pains, you will be closer to your heaven. Do not wish for growth to stop. Keep stretching yourself. Understand that everyone is going through the same process and their behavior may be in an advanced or amateur stage.

It does not matter which stage they are in, but what stage you are in. Look above you always. Seek out the mentor to learn from. You will know who it is because you will feel it is right. It will make sense and it will feel good to you. Your life is your child. Teach it. When you feel you have no choices left, know that your mind is only resisting and playing tricks on you. The resistance is what causes the pain. Tell yourself you do have a choice and no one is going to take that from you.

Slow down and savor life. Study a child and see through their eyes. Watch them look at life as a mystery, asking questions, trying to understand. Pay attention to their ability to visualize, laugh and have fun. How much of this do you do? I believe I have covered most areas that are involved with self-esteem. Read books, go to seminars, and listen to speakers on the Internet or T.V. Study every angle, every belief different than yours and see what may ring true. Try metaphysics, astrology or biorhythms and read about the different philosophies in the world. Drink in the myth and ponder the realities. Absorb more information than you can hold and do not judge what you are absorbing. Do not preach to others, as this is a personal education for you. Let others do their own pursuing. Allow the information to take shape inside you by discerning what works for you and discarding what does not work for you. Remember there will be those that will try to knock you down. Boasting and preaching do no good. Find the proof for yourself. By then you won't need to change anyone because you will begin to realize that everyone else needs to find their own way.

The time will come when you are tested for what you have learned. Your faith in yourself will be the key factor in the test. I guarantee it will not be an easy test, so learn well. Be open to every possibility for growth. The reward will be well worth it. Doubt will be farthest thing from your mind because you will know who you are and what you can handle. No one will be able to throw you off course and if they do, it will not be for long! Life will become a mystery again and not a fear!

Learn to balance your life with fun, play and laughter on a daily basis. Treat yourself to new pleasures. Drive a new way, take a risk and go up in a hot air balloon! Go to the beach or find some puppies to play with you. That is always a great therapy. Find what fun is for you. Try things until you find what it is that inspires you. What is fun for one is not fun always for the other. Seek out those who share similar interests. Be spontaneous to try something different when it seems you resist the most. Who gives you permission, but you? Do not alleviate responsibility in the process, but have fun when you feel you need fun the most. "That was then and this is now and everything has changed!"

Chapter 28
Exercises for Higher Self Esteem

Exercise I—Develop Your Intuition

It is time for some exercises to help you develop some new skills. You already have the ability to develop high self-esteem. As I discussed, self-esteem includes using your inner knower. It is your best therapist if you allow it to come through.

The first thing I would like you to do is buy a coloring book and crayons. Buy the largest box with a sharpener if you like. I would then like you to find the time and the appropriate spot where you feel safe. It also needs to be quiet with absolutely no distractions. Soothing music without people singing or talking is the best so there is no distraction from the coloring. At first, I do not want you to think of anything but coloring. Do not have a talk radio station or T.V. on, as it will distract.

Start coloring. Concentrate on the color combinations and just enjoy the act of coloring. Color as many pictures as you want the way you want. Focus only on what you are doing and forget about everything else.

Pay attention only to how you begin to feel. Are you calming down? Do this as many days as you wish. Do not try to think of anything while you are doing this.

Next, and when you are ready, get a notepad and pen. Lay it next to you on the table. Start coloring and when a thought comes to you, write it down. It does not need to make sense. It can be flash of a thought, an idea, a memory. Go back to coloring again and wait for the next thought. Write it down. It is a form of brainstorming with no perceived direction. These are thoughts that are coming through. They can represent a worry, a desire, a need. Just keep doing this. Do not be afraid of what comes out of your mind. This may help you see what you need to do about something or an area that you might need to take a look at more closely. It could be just a reminder what you are missing with fun.

Take a look at the list after you finish your own therapy session. What does it say to you? Does it make any sense? Is there a pattern? Is it identifying stressors for you?

I would then like you to come up with a question for which you need an answer. This will be aggressive conversation with yourself and your inner knower. Start coloring again and focus only on this question. Just keep coloring until an answer comes to you.

Some people may see a picture instead of hearing a thought. You may get a picture of butterfly hopping from flower to flower. Stop and identify what you feel describes a butterfly. A butterfly is beautiful. It is light and plays around to the joy of those who watch. It starts out as a caterpillar, goes through changes, which are natural, and pops out a completely different life form. This could be a representation of what is happening to you or what needs to happen. Only you know that and your inner knower.

Identify what changes are happening or need to happen to help you be the butterfly. Maybe the other thoughts you have written down will help focus and refine the answer to your question. You should have an understanding of what needs to happen and a direction. The difficulty is not saying "Oh well," but listening to the story your inner knower is telling you. It can be blunt or it will tell you with picture representations.

After a time of doing this, you will be able to harness the ability of getting answers without coloring. Your time will speed up once you become comfortable and have more faith in hearing what is being said. You may eventually get answers from a song or T.V. program, which is on the subject of your question. It could even come out of someone else's mouth.

It will usually be quiet, quick blip of a thought. It will come and go quickly. The goal is to color to help keep your focus on one thing so the clutter of life doesn't get in the way.

If coloring isn't your bag, feel free to put a model airplane together or work in the yard. Whatever relaxes you and puts you in the situation of being alone and relaxed. Have Fun!

Exercise II—What do You Want?
I want you to pick any topic for making a list. Pick several topics, but do only one at a time. For example: My perfect companion, My perfect car, My perfect house, etc.

Make two columns titled "Want" and "Don't Want". This is easier said than done as I can vouch. Let us take the perfect companion. List everything you want in the perfect companion. List everything you don't want in a perfect companion.

You may have to visualize different companions you have dated and pick the traits from them to get started. This will also enable you to see how these people played an important role in your life by helping you identify what you like and don't like.

Once your list is completed, date it and place it somewhere safe and forget about it. As time passes, you will find that you make changes as new people come in and out of your life. By the time you get the list refined, you will know the person when you meet them.

Do this for any topic you wish. Make the list, date it and put it away to view when you remember to look at it. I made some lists once and forgot about them until a year or two later. I looked the list over and found that I did need to refine something and other lists I realized had materialized for me already and it was just as I had listed. You are actually putting energy into the universe and then letting go and letting God process it for you. This is such fun and it works!

Exercise III—Take Your Own Advice

I want you to do some role-playing with yourself in the next exercise. Visualize two chairs in a room. You choose the type chairs and the environment you wish to be in.

You will be the sender and the receiver. Pretend you are the interviewer looking at yourself in the other chair. You are going to ask yourself questions as if you are a person that you have known for awhile.

Question #1: What are your most notable positive traits? *You respond back as if being interviewed on T.V. or radio*
Question # 2: What did you enjoy most as a child?
Question # 3: What kind of a child were you?
Question # 4: How were you taught to deal with anger?
Question # 5: How do you deal with anger now?
   Same or different?
Question # 6: How were you limited as a child?
Question # 7: How are you limited now? Same or different?
Question # 8: What are some favorite things to do if you had the time and money was not an object? What is the obstacle to doing what you want? Has this always been an obstacle as far back as you can remember?
Question # 9: What would it take to eliminate the obstacle?
Question # 10: What advice would you give to you to help eliminate the obstacle?
(Remember) you are talking to someone you care about)
Question # 11: What advice would you give you to help you get on a healthy and happy path?

The key to this exercise is to take the emotion out of this role-playing and talk to the person as if you were giving your best friend some advice. Be honest and think about your answers and try to accept what you hear.

Exercise IV—Affirm Your Problems
List in sentence form all the areas of your life, which you feel are a problem. *For example:* I am depressed everyday. I

can't follow through with any project. I am too giving to others and I have nothing left.

Take each statement and underneath right a positive affirmation for the negative statement. For example: I feel happy and contented everyday because I am where I am supposed to be in my growth. I will finish one project before I start another. I will make sure to give to myself daily, so I can give to others without depleting myself.

Make it fit your problems and your life.

Make a typed list, in big letters if you can, of all the affirmation statements only.

You will eventually not need the problem statements anymore.

Now find a place to post this list or place it in several places. I always suggest on the bathroom mirror, but you pick a place where you will see the affirmations and read through the list. Even if you do not feel like reading it, still force yourself to read it. It takes thirty days to change a habit or a thought process. Just read through the list. You do not have to process the words, but pay attention to what words say. Eliminate any negative tone or sarcasm, as your mind is too smart. If it is an unemotional reading then so be it. Just read in a nonjudgmental manner.

Exercise V—Your Past Influences

The next exercise is to identify your past growth. I would like you to remember back to the first grade in school, which you can remember.

List all of the people you can remember for each specific grade. Identify as many grades and people as you can remember. Write down their name, if you can remember what kind of person they were and then pick something that you learned from them about yourself or about life in general. It can be positive or negative. It can be a classmate or the teacher or someone in neighborhood. It can be someone else's lesson you learned. Maybe you learned something about someone you admired and wanted to be a part of your life. You could have decided what kind of people you liked or disliked.

For example: In first grade, I wore a short-sleeved dress to school in the middle of winter. One of my classmates made a comment, which caused me to withdraw and hide in the coat closet for the first part of the day. The teacher finally found me. I went home for lunch and did not want to return to school. My mother put a sweater on me and the teacher minimized the issue by reinforcing my reading abilities and said nothing about the "catastrophe."

I realized that I was very shy and easily hurt by others. I did not overcome this type of issue at that point in my life, but smacked into similar situations many times before I finally felt I conquered the issue of being easily hurt. I started realizing I could do or be whatever I choose because I was me and I did not need the peer input. I believe it was ninth grade before I finally realized this. I may still be dealing with this, but on a much more enlightened level. So, you see it can take time and many tries to refine a behavioral change in yourself.

In seventh grade, my best friend through grade school turned on me and started trying to make me look bad because she was jealous of the attention I was getting. She wanted to impress our friends. I had not treated her any differently to warrant her behavior change and felt she was still a friend. When I found out what she was doing as my "friend," I immediately eliminated her as a friend. Afterward she denied any such behavior, but I had facts. Over the years this happened many times to me and I had no idea why. I was just being myself and trusting people implicitly. I didn't realize how jealousy made people act.

I learned that your "best friends" or anyone can betray you out of jealousy and insecurity. I realize now it was all part of growing up and I developed the ability to spot this at an early stage. Now I don't allow it to happen if I can see it coming. If it does happen, as soon as I figure it out, and the person denies any such behavior, they are out of my life. I have no time for dishonesty in my life. I will give them the opportunity to at least admit to it and if they don't or can't, I know they are not on my level and they need to learn from someone closer to their level.

It can be enlightening to see how you have evolved, been molded and changed over the years by the people that have been part of your life. You can see what lessons you have learned and how you choose your friends now. Do you still allow people to affect you or have you grown out of the childhood insecurities, which all children go through?

As an example for one of your lists, just simplify the situation: 2nd grade; Sweater issue—Learned I was shy and easily hurt. Out grew this by 9th grade by realizing others are hurtful out of their insecurity and their need to attain favor.
(Be brief for each situation).

Exercise VI—Your Significant Events
The first exercise is necessary for you to create a map of your life. By identifying significant people and situations and the affect on you, whether it was positive or negative. It

can help identify your habits, your likes and dislikes, your developed and undeveloped areas, a significant learning lesson or simply just learning what energies happen to stick in your mind. You may get a chuckle or a warm feeling when you think of them.

The next exercise follows the same system except you are to identify specific situations that were significant to you. Let your mind wander.

I have many, but I will give you an example to help you understand. In seventh grade, my English teacher told us to pick a book and write a book report. I waited until the last night and still had not read a book. So, in my mind, I had only one choice and that was to make one up because I had no time to read. I entitled this book as "Little Kaoula." I have no idea to this day what I created as a plot, but when the paper returned graded, I started to sweat. The teacher said one person did an excellent job and she wanted that person to read their report to the class. When she handed me my papers, it said at the top A+, and asked me to read it to the class. I almost died. I read it to the class and then waited for her to have me produce the book, figuring I was busted. She never did and I carried that secret for a long time for fear of being caught. The point is, I had a gift to write and did not even realize it until my forties. I just knew I could always write and that it was easy for me. It took one of my mentors to bring it back out in me recently as a way for me to utilize my gift combined with my knowledge.

Be brief as you list your significant events. You can simply write:

Seventh grade; "Little Kaoula."

I learned I could write well enough from my own creativity.

I hope you don't feel I have made up this whole book without doing my homework as I do have much background in this area. Just want to alleviate your fears on that thought.

Think of unexplainable situations that happened as well. If it comes to your mind, write it down. This will be your intuition bringing a situation back to your memory banks. Do not ask anyone to help you with these memories at first because these are your significant events, not someone else's. This is your map we are trying to create.

If some of the memories are too painful, then seek counsel to help you deal with the significance. The negative also directs your life and is extremely important to help you heal. It will also help you see where other people were in their growth and how it affected you by their actions and reactions.

Exercise VII—Your Best Friend

The next exercise is easy and you may want to do it with a friend if you so choose. Let's create your best friend. List as many traits as you can think of that you would like to have in a *best friend*. If you have to visualize certain people you know to think of a trait that you like, then do so. Your list should have at least twenty to thirty traits. In groups that I have done this with, it seems to be the norm by the time everyone thinks of their perfect friend.

Once the list is made, look it over and see what you have created. Then notice whether there are any negative traits in the list. My guess is there is not. So far, I haven't seen anyone who truly wants anyone with negative traits for a best friend.

Now look at the list again. This time identify yourself as your very best friend. Be honest as to whether you treat yourself with these same traits. One person looked at me and got a little scared because she had such fun creating her perfect friend, but when she turned the mirror around to herself, she said the list scared her. She said this looked like a whole different list to her now. She admitted to herself and to the group that she did not treat herself with a lot of the characteristics. She did not respect herself; she was not confident, and caring to herself. Each person was able to pick many traits they did not nurture within themselves.

You need to be your own best friend first. How can you expect to be a good friend to someone if your example to yourself doesn't speak very positively? If you are pulling yourself down and judging yourself, your friends will not want you around them because they would prefer their perfect friend to have positive traits as well. In the list you created, the perfect traits need to be directed to yourself. Think about it.

Use the list to start seeing how to change aspects of yourself that will make you the perfect friend...*To you and ultimately to others.*

Exercise VIII—Who Are You Becoming?

Now, take a good look at yourself in the present. I do mean an honest look. The next exercise is to help validate your experiences of the present by looking at your past and then affirming that you are influenced by your past. Know that it still hurts. Other people's behavior in the past did not have an effect on your *real self-esteem* because they were only projecting their self-esteem on to you. And where was their level of self-esteem at the time? Up to a certain age, children are sponges for information and mimic that which they see and hear. They cannot disseminate right and wrong until someone tells them. If the peer's perception is distorted, that person will pass on distorted thinking and actions. What the child experiences becomes "normal" no matter how abnormal it may seem to you and me.

You will need another piece of paper with two columns or you can use two separate pieces of paper. If writing is ever a problem with any of these exercises, you can always tape your words and then play them back.

There will be five categories:
Spiritual, Family, Financial, Social and Physical.

There will be two columns under each category:
    For example:
    One column: *"How I was conditioned,"*
    The other titled: *"What I presently believe"*
Take each category for Spiritual, Family, etc. and place under each column.

    For example:
    Spiritual – *How I was conditioned*
    Spiritual - *What I presently believe.*
    Write as much as you can remember.

Do all of the categories of Spiritual, Family, Financial, Social and Physical the same way. Include all differences and what changed your thinking.

How did you grow from the change? Include positives and negatives from the change so you can see the patterns.

This will be another piece of information to show you that people do evolve and change and it is possible to keep changing and evolving into our own true self in time. How long did it take before changes occurred? Some can take many years. Do not get impatient with yourself now because you had no choice but to evolve the way you did as a child. You resist the changes now because it is a cognitive choice.

Depression starts when you internalize the anger and the pain. It is when your inside esteem does not agree with the outside image. There is conflict between the two. The real you on the inside is fighting the image that others created for you on the outside.

This exercise is to help you see the differences that have been made to date. Keep changing and refining the list every day. Do not stop for anyone. They will either respect you or run from you because they will not be able to control, manipulate or affect you as you get stronger and more confident in who you are becoming. If there are no changes from your conditioning to the present then you are stuck in the past and living someone else's life. This is what is causing your depression.

If it is the same, my suggestion is to start doing one little thing a day that is new for you, even if it is going to get an ice cream cone. Start to find the little things that give you joy. Take the risk to go somewhere new. If you don't like the new experience, then you know you don't need to do that anymore, but you will now *know* you don't like that. Keep experiencing life until you know what you like and dislike. You will be developing your "Self" and not have to listen to everyone else tell you what is good for you or not good for you. You will find that you become stronger and more confident to do things because you will start developing your own beliefs and values.

What one person thinks is right may not be what is right for you. Do not isolate from the world because others think you should be someone they want you to be. Do you want to think and act the way you feel or the way they feel you should think and act?

Parents, wake up! Do not try to plan the life of your child. Only help them to know how to cope with life and allow them to find their own path. That is what makes the world go around! If everyone was a cook, we would have no one to farm and grow the food or someone to market the food. Let everyone find their place in this life and let it be joyous for all!

Exercise IX—Face your Obstacles
List all of the obstacles you feel you have in life at the present. Write as many as you want. It can fill the page if you want. See it with your own eyes. You now have started developing in a direction.

Now go through and prioritize them in the order of importance. Then write beside each one if it is a new problem or one that repeats itself. Just write "new" or "repeat."

Next write if it is controllable by you. Be honest with yourself since most people have the tendency to feel nothing is controllable. It is an emotional or tangible problem?

Now separate the controllable from the non-controllable problems. Set aside the non-controllable problems, as these cannot be resolved without change from someone else. You want to focus only on what you have control over at this time.

Check to see if they are prioritized by importance and if something has changed in priority since you started the list, change it now. If it is an emotional problem, the only thing you can change is a part of you. What part of you needs to change?

What part of the grief process are you stuck in? Shock, Disbelief, Denial, Searching, Bargaining or Acceptance? What will it take for you to accept this problem and let it go? If you are in denial stage of the actual problem, it will continue to manifest over and over.

Take one problem or obstacle, preferably the first on your priority list, and write a clear statement of what is the actual problem. If you cannot identify the actual problem, you are in one of the grief stages. Identify this if you can. Once you can accept that it is a problem you are already releasing some of the energy it has on you.

Looking only at this problem, answer the following questions:

1. Are you too proud to admit there is a problem?
2. Are you too embarrassed to admit you have a problem?
3. What are you trying to protect with this problem?
4. What do you fear will happen if you open this problem up for all to see?
5. Do you need help with this problem?
6. Do you deny that you need help with this problem?
7. Are you using the problem to manipulate others to pay attention to you?
8. What patterns of reoccurrence do you see, if any?

9. Is this a problem that has been passed down to you and you think it is your problem as well?

10. Do you want to keep experiencing the consequences of this problem?

11. Does the problem need to be resolved at this time?

12. Do you have the capabilities and/or contacts to initiate change of the problem?

Are you ready to let go of the problem or are you comfortable being uncomfortable? If you feel you have had enough of this problem and you have accepted that you want to solve this problem after dissecting it with the answers to the above questions, you have a few choices to make.

You have the problem or obstacle written down. List all of the alternatives you can think of for this one issue. Solicit alternatives from others if you choose, but do not internalize their opinions; just add them to your list. Ask someone you respect.

Now use the method I discussed about making decisions using your own intuition.

The two most powerful questions:

Will this alternative make me feel weak, tense, and unsure, if I choose this way? Will this alternative make me feel free, strong, and more sure, if I choose this way? Pay attention to your body and how it responds to the questions you ask it.

Remember, if you feel frustrated using this method, try an old problem that has already been resolved and you know the correct answer. Then ask the questions again after you remember the feelings. Practice this method until you can whiz right through the alternatives to the correct answer by *feeling* the answer. If there is no distinct answer yet, that means it is not the time yet. Go on to the next problem or obstacle and use the same method. Sometimes the answer will come when you least expect it. Be patient with your intuition because as I said, if you are too stressed, it will not fight its way through. It will find a breach in the barrier and pop it through when you can accept it. Be patient. If the answers do not come, let it go for now, and go on to the next situation. Sometimes the answer is to do nothing. That is hard for us to accept because we always feel we need to do something.

The bottom line to this is write your issue down, separate them into what you can control yourself, prioritize them, answer the list of questions to see where you are with the issue, choose one issue that you are ready to resolve, and try the method of using your own intuition through the feeling in your body to get your own answers. Make sure when you are using the intuitive method that you are by yourself in a place that is peaceful to you and no clutter of noises to distract you.

Do not try to solve more than one problem at a time as this is when people get overwhelmed and give up. You will be creating a direction for yourself by solving even the smallest problem. Try taking one each day to work on and concentrate only on that one. At the end of the work day, let it go and do something enjoyable for yourself. The energy you have put toward it will vibrate through the universe and come back to you when it is time.

This is the same concept as writing something down and putting it aside and forgetting about it. The energy will start working on its own and you can enjoy some life knowing that you have put your best energy out there. Let go and let God now.

Chapter 29
Be On Your Way

In a perfect world, you should have all of your lists com-pleted and all of your data surrounding you. You should know your past very well and all of the situations and people that have affected you and molded you as you are now. You should be able to see the differences and changes you have made along the way and note the attitude, guilt and belief of those who trained you and what you have changed or kept as part of you.

You have learned that the grief process and identification of personal obstacles is actually a natural part of your growth if you can accept it and face it. You should understand that you are in the mess you are in because you have believed and accepted that the answers of other people were right for you. You have come to believe in fear and fear is simply not know-ing. You have some new methods to allow your own intuition to help you through your stresses, but you need to remember that you are made up of three parts. You need a balance of spiritual, mental and the physical. When one is missing, you feel the void of missing something that is keeping you from being fulfilled. The spiritual will guide you through the men-tal and then to the physical. So develop and become friends with that part of you first.

Increase your awareness by experiencing as much as you can. Use your imagination and visualization to keep your mental muscles strong. Do not try to drag any one down or limit their growth because that only means that you are below them. If you are happy and feel your life is perfect, then there is no reason to change. If you want different people around you and different things, then you need to allow the changes. You can't make the changes until you experience what you like and dislike or what you want and don't want. Your freedom will come when your choice comes from within you and not from someone else.

Listen to yourself. It is not a perfect world. Everyone is evolving at different rates and who is demanding the perfection? Has anyone achieved the ultimate perfection? Remember the saying "Green apples grow and ripe apples rot!" To those who feel that they have reached the very top will find out there is another mountain on the other side.

Taking one step at a time and one problem at a time is all that is expected. If you try to deal with all that has been dealt to you at once, you would certainly be overwhelmed and very depressed. I would be happy if you did one of the lists. This would be a beginning for your new awareness. The idea of having to forgive yourself for all that has happened and the guilt that has been created by others, I feel is somewhat ludicrous. You only need to accept yourself and others for all of the experiences that come your way, learn from them, change them and rearrange them to find your balance. You only did what you knew to do at the time. There are no right or wrong answers.

Don't be afraid to ask for help. I was taught to do things for myself and by myself. That caused me to lose a lot of time because I did do most things by myself without help when it came to the mental growth. That was not easy believe me! I was making mistakes well into my adulthood that could have been handled at an earlier age if I had asked for the appropriate help. I spent years in confusion and kept hearing the same thing in my head "You have to do it by yourself. Don't ask anyone for help."

How can you figure something out without any awareness or new data. I guess this is why I became so obsessed in learning because I only had myself to count on. As they say in business: "90% preparation and 10% presentation". This is with your own life as well. Let go of the things you can't change. Be prepared to accept the critiques of ourselves. *These are the pearls you need to begin change.*

The more you know about yourself, the less people will be able to control, manipulate or affect your self esteem. Do not be afraid of self-esteem. It is only the many experiences you have that mold who you are and who you want to become. It is your core. It is you. It is knowing that you know.

Our first love and last love is self love—Bovee
Have faith in yourself and your faith will be rewarded many times over.

My best to all of you on your journey;
My best to God for guiding me safely on my journey.
Joanne

ABOUT THE
AUTHOR

Joanne Salsbury was born in Portsmouth, Ohio. It is a small southern Ohio River town that is nestled in a state forest with prominent Indian heritage. She grew up knowing the land and the peace it can bring as well as the education of life beyond the books. She gained education in Europe and finalized her degrees at the University of Cincinnati.

Presently, she is living in San Diego, California where she is in hospital administration. Joanne had her own business for twelve years as a consultant in restructuring of companies with a goal of achieving high self esteem businesses. She has done extensive public speaking and seminars for the individual as well as for companies.

Joanne is writing to all of the people in the world in hopes that each person realizes that he/she can achieve high self esteem no matter of your education, circumstances or background. High self-esteem is a personal issue between you and your higher good. It is learned behavior that is compiled from all of your experiences and interactions and refined over time to paint that picture of yourself that you can love unconditionally.

Our natural emotions have been distorted in value over time and she would like to help you remember and gain back the understanding and purpose of your own emotions, so you can have your own self esteem back as well.

www.ingramcontent.com/pod-product-compliance
Lightning Source LLC
Chambersburg PA
CBHW070205060426
42445CB00033B/1543